VERBAL PLENARY PRESERVATION

OF THE BIBLE

A Course On The Bible's Doctrine Of Verbal Plenary Preservation

Rev. Dennis Kwok,
Pastor of Truth Bible- Presbyterian Church
&
The Faculty of Far Eastern Bible College

Editor: H. D. Williams, M.D., Ph. D.

Published by
The Old Paths Publications, Inc.

For: Bible For Today Ministries &
The Dean Burgon Society

Disclaimer

The authors of this work have quoted the writers of many articles and books. This does not mean that the authors endorse or recommend the works of others. If an author quotes someone, it does not mean that he agrees with all of the author's tenets, statements, concepts, or words, whether in the work quoted or any other work of the author. There has been no attempt to alter the meaning of the quotes; and therefore, some of the quotes are long in order to give the entire sense of the passage.

Library of Congress Control Number: 2008935766

REL006050 Religion: Biblical Commentary – General.

ISBN 978-0-9817985-4-7

All Scripture quotes are from the King James Bible except those verses compared and then the source is identified.

Address All Inquiries To:
THE OLD PATHS PUBLICATIONS, Inc.
142 Gold Flume Way
Cleveland, Georgia, U.S.A. 30528

Web: www.theoldpathspublications.com
E-mail: TOP@theoldpathspublications.com

BIBLE FOR TODAY #3376
Web: www.bibffortoday.org
E-mail: bft@biblefortoday.org

DEAN BURGON SOCIETY
Web: www.deanburgonsociety.org

Cover Design: Patricia Williams

1.0

PREFACE

The Battle in the Past. For many years (or even centuries), ever since the serpent said, "*Yea, hath God said*" (Genesis 3:1), there has been a questioning of the fact of, the extent of, and the manner of Bible preservation. In this book, the editor, Dr. H. D. Williams, has reproduced in one volume these truths that had been previously made available in ten separate lessons. Through the permission of Dr. Jeffrey Khoo, the Dean of the Far Eastern Bible College (FEBC) in Singapore, and the other authors, we have been able to make these important studies available to the entire English-speaking world in book form. Dr. Khoo and his fundamental Bible Presbyterian associates have paid a tremendous price in standing for the verbal plenary preservation of the Words of the Bible.

The Battle in the Present.. As this book is being published, the FEBC, which holds to the sound position of the verbal plenary preservation of the Bible, has been asked either to give up this Biblical position, or to move out of the buildings they have occupied since their beginning. Those who have ordered them out of their school properties are the leaders of the Life Bible Presbyterian Church, formerly pastored by Dr. Timothy Tow, until his forced resignation over this truth. Dr. Tow and his brother, Dr. S. H. Tow (President of the FEBC board of directors) have been seeking to solve this crisis by conciliatory means but to no avail.

The Battle in the Future. The removal of FEBC from their former quarters is a matter yet to be decided as of this writing, but the battle for the truth of the verbal plenary preservation of the Words of God will go on until the coming of our Lord Jesus Christ. In the United States, opposition comes not only from the Roman Catholic Church, the apostate Protestants, and the compromising New Evangelicals, but also, sadly, even from many leading Fundamentalists, fundamental churches, and fundamental schools. The leading schools that oppose this Biblical teaching include Bob Jones University, Detroit Baptist Seminary, Central Baptist Seminary, Calvary Baptist Seminary, and many of their sister schools. "*Verbal*" refers to the Words, not merely the ideas, concepts, thoughts, or message. "*Plenary*" refers to the entire Bible from Genesis to Revelation. "*Preservation*" refers to the inerrant preservation of the original Hebrew, Aramaic, and Greek Words from their verbal plenary inspiration to this present hour.

Sincerely yours for God's Words,
Pastor D. A. Waite, Th.D., Ph.D.,
President of the Bible For Today, and
President of the Dean Burgon Society

TABLE OF CONTENTS

ABBREVIATIONS

BFT = Bible For Today
CEV = Contemporary English Version
CUV – Chinese Union Version
DBS = Dean Burgon Society
ESV = English Standard Version
FEBC = Far Eastern Bible College
KJB = King James Bible
LB = Living Bible
LBPC = Life Bible Presbyterian Church
NASB = New American Standard Version
NIV = New International Version
NLB = New Living Bible
RSV = Revised Standard Version
TBPC = Truth Life Bible Presbyterian Church
TEV – Today's English Version
VPI = verbal plenary inspiration
VPP = verbal plenary preservation
WCF = Westminster Confession of Faith
W/H = Westcott and Hort

COURSE DESCRIPTION

The following course on verbal plenary preservation (VPP) of the Hebrew, Aramaic, and Greek Words that lie behind the King James Bible is taught at the Far Eastern Bible College (FEBC) and Truth Bible-Presbyterian Church (TBPC) in Singapore. It is printed with their permission. The Dean Burgon Society (DBS) and Bible For Today Baptist Ministries (BFT) highly recommends it for those who desire the truth behind the modern conundrum of Bible texts, the 'new' versions of the Bible, and the mass confusion surrounding these topics.

I. COURSE DESCRIPTION

This course is on the doctrine of Verbal Plenary Preservation (VPP) of the Bible. It will discuss the inspiration, canonicity, identification, transmission and translation of Scripture that support fully the doctrine of VPP. VPP is a biblical doctrine that is well-supported by the Scriptures. The superiority of the King James Bible and the Textus Receptus that underlies it will also be demonstrated.

II. RECOMMENDED TEXTS

1. D A Waite, *Defending the King James Bible* (Collingswood NJ: The Bible for Today Press, 1994).

2. Dean J W Burgon, *The Revision Revised: A Refutation of Westcott and Hort's False Greek Text and Theory* (Collingswood NJ: Dean Burgon Society Press).

3. Edward F Hills, *The King James Version Defended* (Des Moines IA: The Christian Research Press, 1984).

4. Jeffrey Khoo, *Kept Pure in All Ages: Recapturing the Authorized Version and the Doctrine of Providential Preservation* (Singapore: FEBC Press, 2001).

5. S H Tow, *Beyond Versions* (Singapore: King James Productions, 1998).

6. Timothy Tow & Jeffrey Khoo, *A Theology for Every Christian Book I: Knowing God & His Word* (Singapore: FEBC Press, 1998).

III. Lessons

Lesson No.	Topic	Author/Teacher
Lesson 1	Introduction to the Doctrine of VPP	Dennis Kwok
Lesson 2	Inspiration & VPP	Dennis Kwok
Lesson 3	Biblical Support for VPP (I)	Carol Lee
Lesson 4	Biblical Support for VPP (II)	Quek Suan Yew
Lesson 5	Biblical Support for VPP (III)	Quek Suan Yew
Lesson 6	Biblical Support for VPP (IV)	Das Koshy
Lesson 7	The King James Bible & VPP	Dennis Kwok
Lesson 8	Identification of God's Preserved Words (I)	Jeffrey Khoo
Lesson 9	Identification of God's Preserved Words (II)	Jeffrey Khoo
Lesson 10	Conclusion / Q & A Session	All teachers

Links to more articles on the defense of VPP are at the end of this course.

LESSON 1

INTRODUCTION

To The Doctrine Of
Verbal Plenary Preservation

I. DEFINITION OF VPP

What does VPP mean? "Verbal" means "every word to the jot and tittle" (Ps 12:6-7, Matt 5:18). "Plenary" means "the Scripture as a whole with all the words intact" (Matt 24:35, 1 Pet 1:25). So VPP means the whole of Scripture with all its words even to the jot and tittle is perfectly preserved by God without any loss of the original words, prophecies, promises, commandments, doctrines, and truths, not only in the words of salvation, but also the words of history, geography and science. Every book, every chapter, every verse, every word, every syllable, every letter is infallibly preserved by the Lord Himself to the last iota.

II. THE BEGINNINGS OF VPP ISSUE IN SINGAPORE

A. Two Deadly Poisons: *'From The Mind of God to the Mind of Man'* and *'One Bible Only?'*

1. The battle to be fought today is the battle for the Bible. The doctrine of inspiration was fought in the last century. In this new century, it is the battle of the doctrine of Bible preservation. Far Eastern Bible College of Singapore stood firm on God's providential preservation of the perfect Bible and is still standing today without compromise and apology.

2. The book 'From the Mind of God to the Mind of Man' published by Bob Jones University in 1999 attacks the fundamental doctrine of Bible preservation by having an inclination to the critical texts originated from Westcott and Hort. In addition, BJU adopts a neutral position on the

English Bible versions. This is the first poison that spreads to all who adore BJU as one Bible seminary and university that stood without apology through the dangerous time of great apostasy. Unfortunately, like many other Bible seminaries which had fallen, BJU succumbed to the god of humanistic scholarship and downgraded spiritual and biblical discernment. Thus, FEBC, being true to her call to be God's watchman in these last of the last days, must sound the alarm bell of warning.

3. The second poison is found in the book 'One Bible Only?' which was written by the Baptist fundamentalists who taught at Central Baptist Theological Seminary of Plymouth, Minnesota. This book speaks in one voice throughout saying that the Bible is preserved conceptually, and not verbally. In other words, it was believed that only the vital doctrines are preserved, and not the inspired words. Many of the non-VPPists or anti-VPPists sing the same tune as this book. Their arguments against the doctrine of VPP are relatively the same.

B. Life BPC & FEBC

1. Dr Jeffrey Khoo, the Academic Dean of FEBC, wrote two separate critiques against the two poison books which were highly endorsed by BJU and Central Baptist Seminary, in order to defend the King James Bible and the original language texts underlying it. His timely critiques serve as a strong warning to the readers of these books. The teaching of the doctrine of VPP has thus taken root and eventually became the hot topic among B-P churches in Singapore

2. Among the teaching faculty members of FEBC, two disagreed on the doctrine of VPP. As a result, they resigned from the faculty but remained as assistant pastors of Life BPC. Due to their influence and good support from the Church Session, Life BPC steered a different direction from FEBC. Since then, anti-VPP statements were consistently made and taught that VPP is a new teaching and remains a personal conviction rather than a universal gospel truth.

3. Thus, Life BPC and FEBC went on separate ways from the last quarter of 2003 onwards. In the same year, FEBC Principal Rev Timothy Tow resigned from Life BPC as pastor and started a new church called 'True Life BPC' under the umbrella of FEBC.

C. Calvary BPC & Truth BPC

"Truth will out' is what Rev Timothy Tow always reminded his students in FEBC. The issue of VPP did not remain with Life-FEBC. For more than two years, Calvary BPC has been staying clear of this sensitive issue for fear of splitting the church. It was until 2 Oct 2005, an official church stand was made for a non-VPP position, though not without a strong appeal made to the Board of Elders against making such a hasty decision. As a result, five deacons and two full-time staffworkers, unwilling to submit to a non-VPP stand, resigned from their offices at the end of the year 2005. It was in such a situation, Truth BPC was born on 1 Jan 2006 at Calvary Pandan BPC premises to take a firm stand on the doctrine of VPP. "For we can do nothing against the truth but for the truth" (2 Cor 13:8).

III. THE IMPORTANCE OF VPP

A. Inspiration and Preservation are Twin Brothers!

1. Non-VPPists or anti-VPPists do not believe the God who perfectly inspired His Word has also perfectly preserved His Word. They affirm Verbal Plenary Inspiration (VPI) but deny Verbal Plenary Preservation (VPP). They believe strongly that we do not have an infallible and inerrant Bible TODAY and thereby their denial of the doctrine of VPP. By denying VPP, they might as well deny VPI, for what is the use of an infallible and inerrant Bible in the past but not today?

2. Dr Ian Paisley was absolutely correct to say, "The verbal Inspiration of the Scriptures demands the verbal Preservation of the Scriptures. Those who would deny the need for verbal Preservation cannot be accepted as committed to verbal Inspiration. If there is no preserved Word of God today then the work of Divine Revelation and Divine Inspiration has perished" (My Plea for the Old Sword, 103).

3. Dr Timothy Tow, founding pastor of the Bible-Presbyterian Church in Singapore and principal of the Far Eastern Bible College, likewise wrote, "We believe the preservation of Holy Scripture and its Divine inspiration stand in the same position as providence and creation. If Deism teaches a Creator who goes to sleep after creating the world is absurd, to hold to the doctrine of inspiration without preservation is equally illogical. ... Without preservation, all the inspiration, God-breathing into the Scriptures, would be lost. But we have a Bible so pure and powerful in every word and it is so because God has preserved it down through the ages" (A Theology for Every Christian: Knowing God and His Word, 47).

4. Dr Hills wrote, "If the doctrine of *divine inspiration* of the Old and New Testament Scriptures is a true doctrine, the doctrine of the *providential preservation* of these Scriptures must also be a true doctrine. It must be that down through the centuries God has exercised a special, providential control over the copying of the Scriptures and the preservation and use of the original text have been available to God's people in every age. God must have done this, for if He gave the Scriptures to His Church by inspiration as the perfect and final revelation of His will, then it is obvious that He would not allow this revelation to disappear or undergo any alteration of its fundamental character" (*The King James Version* Defended, 2).

B. The Doctrine of Bible Preservation is not a New Teaching!

1. The doctrine of the 100% inspiration and 100% preservation of God's Holy Word existed even before the Westminster Confession as much as the doctrine of the 100% deity and 100% humanity of Christ existed before the Athanasian Creed. The doctrine of 100% inspiration and 100% preservation of God's words in the Holy Scriptures is not a new doctrine but a very old one. It certainly did not begin with D A Waite, nor E F Hills, nor J W Burgon, but with the Holy Scripture itself.

2. The doctrine of preservation is as old as the Bible. Why is the Bible our Supreme, Final, and All-sufficient Authority in faith and life? It is precisely because it is God's Perfect Word, infallible and inerrant, even today!

C. The Doctrine of VPP is Biblical!

1. The *Westminster Confession of Faith* (WCF) states very clearly that the inspired Scriptures in the original languages are by God's "singular care and providence, kept pure in all ages" (WCF I:8). The Westminster divines used Matthew 5:18 as a proof text for this affirmation of the verbal plenary preservation (VPP) of the Scriptures. This proves that the doctrine of the VPP of Scripture is not just creedal, but more importantly *Biblical*.

2. The VPP of Scripture is a position of faith that is based solely on the Word of God. "*Now faith is the substance of things hoped for, the evidence of things not seen*" (Heb 11:1). "*So then faith cometh by hearing, and hearing by the word of God*" (Rom 10:17). "*But without faith it is impossible to please him: for he that cometh to God must believe that he is, and that he is a rewarder of them that diligently*

seek him" (Heb 11:6). It is a position that we must take if we are to weather and survive the onslaughts of postmodernism, pop-modernism, open-theism and neo-deism that seek to destroy the church today.

D. What Kind of Bible Preservation?

1. Many including non-VPPists say they believe in providential preservation. This is what they say, but what do they really mean? Non-VPPist will tell you he believes in preservation, however he does not mean entire preservation but essential preservation; it is conceptual preservation, not verbal preservation. In other words, he believes that only the vital doctrines are preserved and not the inspired words.

2. Does the Bible teach partial and conceptual preservation or plenary and verbal preservation? The Bible and the Protestant Church creeds affirm the latter. The Reformed Confessions in both Presbyterian and Baptist circles affirm not just the 100% inspiration of the Autographs, but also the 100% preservation of the Autographs in the faithful Apographs that have come down to us today.

3. The Westminster Confession of Faith (1.8) for instance states, "*The Old Testament in Hebrew (which was the native language of the people of God of old), and the New Testament in Greek (which, at the time of the writing of it, was most generally known to the nations), being immediately inspired by God, and, by His singular care and providence, kept pure in all ages, are therefore authentical; so as, in all controversies of religion, the Church is finally to appeal unto them.*" Note that the Westminster Confession did not use the term "Autographs" but spoke of the Scriptures in terms of the original languages (Hebrew OT and Greek NT). The Westminster Confession clearly affirms the 100% inspiration ("immediately inspired by God") and 100% preservation ("by His singular care and providence, kept pure in all ages") of the Holy Scriptures in the original languages.

E. What and Where are the Preserved Texts Today?

1. They are the inspired OT Hebrew words and NT Greek words the prophets, the apostles, the church fathers, the reformers used which are today found in the long and continuously abiding and preserved words underlying the Reformation Bibles best represented by the time-tested and time-honoured KJB, and **NOT** in the corrupted Alexandrian

manuscripts and critical Westcott-Hort texts underlying the liberal, ecumenical, and neo-evangelical modern English versions.

2. To be more precise, the infallible and inerrant words of Scripture are found in the faithfully preserved Traditional/Byzantine/Majority manuscripts, and fully represented in the Printed and Received Text (or Textus Receptus) that underlie the Reformation Bibles best represented by the KJB, and **NOT** in the corrupted and rejected texts of Westcott and Hort that underlie the many modern versions of the English Bible like the NIV, NASV, ESV, RSV,TEV, CEV, etc.

F. Are there Scribal/Copyist Mistakes?

1. We do not deny that copying mistakes were made during the transcription process, but that does not negate the fact that God has superintended the transcription of His inspired words to ensure that none of His inspired words would be lost. If 10 scribes were copying the Scriptures, one or two might possibly make a mistake in copying a particular verse, but the rest would have copied it correctly, and the mistake made is easily identified and rectified by the rest. The special providential hand of God has ensured this.

2. God's providential work is always supernatural. God knows all things and is all-powerful. Man makes mistakes, but not God. He who has inspired every jot and tittle of His Word has surely preserved every jot and tittle of His Word (Matt 5:18).

3. There are no mistakes in the Bible. If there are any "discrepancies" in the Bible, the "discrepancies" are only seeming or apparent, **NOT** real or actual. Any inability to understand or explain such difficult passages in no way negates the infallibility and inerrancy of the Scriptures, applying the faithful Pauline principle of biblical interpretation: " *let God be true, but every man a liar*" (Rom 3:4)

G. Is KJB Inspired?

1. Anti-VPPists are prone to put words into the mouths of VPP proponents by saying that they believe the KJB to be as inspired and as infallible and inerrant as the original language Scriptures. We make no such claim. We believe that "the King James Version (or Authorized Version) of the English Bible is a *true, faithful, and accurate* translation of these two providentially preserved Texts [Traditional Masoretic Hebrew Text and Traditional Greek Text underlying the KJB], which in

our time has no equal among all of the other English Translations. The translators did such a fine job in their translation task that we can without apology hold up the Authorized Version and say 'This is the Word of God!' while at the same time realising that, in some verses, *we must go back to the underlying original language Texts* for complete clarity, and also compare Scripture with Scripture" (*The Dean Burgon Society, "Articles of Faith," section II.A*).

2. No translation can claim to be 100% equivalent to the original language Scriptures, but if it is a true, faithful, accurate translation based on the preserved text, it is the Word of God. The Textus Receptus is like the platinum yardstick of the Smithsonian Institute, accurate to the last decimal point. The KJB on the other hand is like the wooden yardstick used in the homes and shops. Would anyone deny that the common yardstick though not the perfect yardstick of the Smithsonian Institute is any less a yardstick and fit to measure?' (Dr Jeffrey Khoo, *The Emergence of Neo-Fundamentalism: One Bible Only? Or Yea Hath God Said?*, January Issue of Burning Bush Volume 10 Number 1).

3. Many English versions have been published, but none has yet overthrown the KJB. The KJB remains the best, most faithful, reliable, accurate, trustworthy, beautiful English Bible we have today. Can the venerable KJB ever be replaced? Should we ever think of revising it? Here is Dean Burgon's reply: "Whatever may be urged in favour of Biblical Revision, it is at least undeniable that the undertaking involves a tremendous risk. Our Authorized Version is the one religious link which at present binds together ... millions of English-speaking men scattered over the earth's surface. Is it reasonable that so unutterably precious, so sacred a bond should be endangered, for the sake of representing certain words more accurately,—here and there translating a tense with greater precision,—getting rid of a few archaisms? It may be confidently assumed that no 'Revision' of our Authorized Version, however judiciously executed, will ever occupy the place in public esteem which is actually enjoyed by the work of the Translators of 1611,—the noblest literary work in the Anglo-Saxon language. We shall in fact never have *another* 'Authorized Version'" (*Revision Revised*, 113).

IV. SUMMARY

Our earnest contention for the inerrancy and infallibility of an extant Bible in the original languages is not an act of schism but of love for both God and man. We are intent on teaching *"all the counsel of God"* (Acts 20:27); we can do no less. The doctrine of VPP promotes God and glorifies Him, for it testifies of His character as One who is the same yesterday, today and forever. He means what He says, and says what He means. *"Heaven and earth shall pass away, but My WORDS shall not pass away"* (Matt 24:35). Is this divine statement not clear enough?

Dr Jeffrey Khoo in his critique (published in FEBC Burning Bush Volume 10 Number 1) of the book One Bible Only? wrote 'Hindus and Muslims all believe that their scriptures, the Bhagavad Gita and the Koran respectively, are perfect. Yet Christians who claim to believe in the one living and true God, the Creator of heaven and earth, and Christ the only Mediator and Saviour of the world, are not so quick to believe they have an existing infallible and inerrant Scripture. What a shame!' If we adopt a non-VPP position, then Christianity is no longer true, and Christians shall become the laughing stock of the religious world. Indeed, if the Christian Bible is not perfect, infallible and inerrant today and it is a thing of the past, *"then is our preaching vain, and your faith is also vain. Yea, and we are found false witnesses of God; ... If in this life only we have hope in Christ, we are of all men most miserable"* (1 Cor 15:14-15, 19).

Basically, those who hold to the VPP of Scripture believe and embrace the following tenets:

1. God has supernaturally preserved each and every one of His inspired Hebrew/Aramaic OT words and Greek NT words to the last jot and tittle, so that in every age, God's people will always have in their possession His infallible and inerrant Word kept intact without the loss of any word (Ps 12:6-7, Matt 5:18, 24:35, Mark 13:31, Luke 21:33, John 10:35, 1 Pet1:23-25).

2. The "providential" preservation of Scriptures is understood as God's special and not general providence. *Special* providence or *providentia extraordinaria* speaks of God's miraculous intervention in the events of history and in the affairs of mankind in fulfilment of His sovereign will for the sake of His elect and to the glory of His Name. The divine

preservation of the Canon (books) and Text (words) of Scripture comes under God's *special* providence.

3. The Bible is not only infallible and inerrant in the past (in the Autographs), but also infallible and inerrant today (in the Apographs).

4. The infallible and inerrant words of Scripture are found in the faithfully preserved Traditional/Byzantine/Majority manuscripts, and fully represented in the Printed and Received Text (or Textus Receptus) that underlie the Reformation Bibles best represented by the KJB, and **NOT** in the corrupted and rejected texts of Westcott and Hort that underlie the many modern versions of the English Bible like the NIV, NASV, ESV, RSV, TEV, CEV, etc.

5. There are no mistakes in the Bible, period. There are no mistakes or errors (scribal or otherwise) in such OT passages as Judges 18:30, 1 Samuel 13:1, 1 Kings 4:26, 1 Chronicles 18:3, 2 Chronicles 22:2 etc. If there are "discrepancies" in the Bible, the "discrepancies" are only seeming or apparent, **NOT** real or actual. Any inability to understand or explain such difficult passages in no way negates the infallibility and inerrancy of the Scriptures, applying the faithful Pauline principle of biblical interpretation: "*let God be true, but every man a liar*" (Rom 3:4).

6. Knowing where the perfect Bible is is a matter of textual recognition and **NOT** textual criticism. In the field of textual recognition, Burgon is good, Hills is better, Waite is best.

7. The Chinese Union Version (CUV) is the "Word of God" for the Chinese people today since it is the best, most faithful, most reliable, and most accurate version among the Chinese versions presently available. Great care ought to be taken not to undermine our Chinese brethren's confidence in the CUV. Nevertheless, versions or translations are never superior to the inspired and preserved Hebrew, Aramaic and Greek Scriptures; thus there is a need to consult these original language Scriptures for clarity and fulness of meaning, and to compare Scripture with Scripture.

LESSON 2

INSPIRATION AND VPP

I. DEFINITION OF INSPIRATION

A. Meaning of Inspiration

1. The Bible is God-breathed. *"All scripture is given by inspiration of God..."* (2 Tim 3:16). The word *inspiration* is translated from a compound Greek word (theo-pnuestos) which means 'God-breathed.' Thus this verse says that 'all Scripture is God-breathed.' God directly breathed out His words over a period of about 1,500 years to approximately 40 specially chosen men of God who wrote them down to give us our Scriptures, the Word of God in three languages (Hebrew, Aramaic and Greek).

2. With so many human writers, one is more inclined to think there would a total diversity or contrary opinions within the writings. However, there is an undisputable consistency of theme, a thread of continuity and unity from Genesis to Revelation. It is as though there were collusion among these writers, spanning nearly 1,500 years to produce something flawless and inspiring. The conclusion must be that there was a single mind and therefore the author behind the writings in which formed the Book is the Almighty God. The Bible is clear in revealing that God is the Author of the Bible (see Ps 68:11; Heb 1:1; 1 Cor 2:13; Gal 1:11-12; etc).

3. The inspiration of the Bible was a direct and unique act of the Holy Spirit and cannot be duplicated by man. The process of inspiration is a mystery of the providence of God, but the result of the process is a Book preserved and authorized made available to us today.

B. Meaning of Verbal Inspiration

1. This [Bible] is the writing of the living God: each letter was penned with an Almighty finger; each word in it dropped from the everlasting lips; each sentence was dictated by the Holy Spirit.' – C. H. Spurgeon

2. The word *verbal* means 'by means of words,' or 'word for word.' As used of inspiration, it means the very words of the Bible were breathed out by God. In other words, God gave the **exact words** of Scripture (see 2 Sam 23:2; Acts 1:16; 1 Cor 2:13).

3. The testimony of Jesus in Matt 5:18 says, *"For verily I say unto you, Till heaven and earth pass, one jot or one tittle shall in no wise pass from the law, till all be fulfilled."* A "jot" is the smallest letter of the Hebrew Alphabet (yod י). A "tittle" is a small appendage that differentiates between two similar-looking letters in the alphabet (beth ב as compared to kaph כ).

C. Meaning of Verbal Plenary Inspiration

1. Every word of the Bible is God-breathed. "It is written, Man shall not live by bread alone, but by every word that proceedeth out of the mouth of God" (Matt 4:4).

2. The word plenary means 'full.' Of inspiration, it means that the 'full' Bible is inspired, or that every word is breathed out by God (see Prov 30:5).

'That this inspiration should extend to the very words seems most natural since the purpose of inspiration is to secure an infallible record of truth. Thoughts and words are so inseparably connected that as a rule a change in words means a change in thought.' – Loraine Boettner

II. THE MIRACULOUS WORK OF DIVINE INSPIRATION

A. Holy Men Set Apart and Prepared by God to Write the Scripture

1. *For the prophecy came not in old time by the will of man: but holy men of God spake as they were moved by the Holy Ghost"* (2 Pet 1:21). God would not trust His holy Word to unregenerate men, for how can they touch the Holy Thing of God without a clean hand and a pure heart? Although the 40 men were not perfect, they had a deep reverence for God and were considered spiritual leaders of their day (see the complete list of the writers of Scripture in the Appendix 1).

2. God prepared these 40 men, using and transcending their personalities, for the writing of His Word. Some of them were leaders, musicians, teachers, and from all walks of life. Since God is the

Creator of language and the Master of all styles, He could give His Word in the styles of David, Jeremiah, Peter, Paul and the rest of them, all exhibit unique styles, when inspired by the Holy Spirit to pen down His Word.

3. And when they wrote, since it is the Holy Spirit who guided them, wrote exactly what men are: sinners in need of salvation. Sins were exposed, revealed, shamed and punished. The Bible did not ignore Moses' anger, David's sin of adultery, or Peter's denial of his Lord three times. Sinful men left to themselves could never have written a book so revealing of human nature.

B. Non-eyewitnesses to Write the Scripture

1. In Genesis 1 God described the Creation of the world. He gave that information to mankind through Moses. But neither Moses nor any other human being was an eyewitness to Creation. God breathed into Moses the description of something Moses knew nothing about.

2. Daniel admitted that he did not understand what he was writing (see Dan 12:8-9). Certainly God does not require the writers to see or understand in order to pen down His Word since it is His Word which is to be written and not theirs.

C. Eyewitnesses to Write the Scripture

However God did inspire some of these men to write those things which they had been eyewitnesses. *"That which was from the beginning, which we have heard, which we have seen with our eyes, which we have looked upon, and our hands have handled, of the Word of life; ... That which we have seen and heard declare we unto you, that ye also may have fellowship with us"* (1 John 1:1-3).

III. THE FALSE VIEWS OF INSPIRATION

A. Natural Inspiration

This false idea teaches that man can reach high levels of creativity like Shakespeare, Bach or Beethoven and equate with 'inspiration' to write the Bible. This modernistic idea teaches inspiration without God but exalted man to develop inspiration naturally on his own. This type of 'inspiration' is certainly fallible since it derived from sinful man.

B. Partial Inspiration

1. This false teaching claims that the Bible merely 'contains' the Word of God. It claims that some of the Bible is inspired, and not all; the Bible may be accurate in morals and doctrine, but unreliable in areas of science, geography and history.

2. This view ultimately makes man the final authority in determining which passages are inspired and which are not. Anytime a fallible human being becomes the judge and final authority, the Bible in his hand becomes no more his supreme and the only authority. If the Bible is truly God's Word as it claims, then it must be perfect by definition (since the product of a perfect God can be nothing less than perfect).

3. If the Bible is accurate in areas of major importance, why should it not be accurate also in areas of minor importance? We realize that all of the Bible is important, but those who believe in this teaching say that we can only trust it on the issues of eternal life, salvation, etc. Don't fall into the trap of the evil one! If we can trust the Bible for our eternal destiny, we can also trust it to be accurate in every area of life and thought.

C. Conceptual Inspiration

1. This unscriptural idea says that God only inspired the thoughts of the Bible and man wrote those thoughts down in his own words. It rejects verbal plenary inspiration, saying it is unbelievable to imagine God dictating every Word. But whose words is greater, God's or man's; the Creator's or the creature's? God said it, I believe it, that settles it!

2. Thoughts were not written down, but words. It is impossible to have wordless thoughts. If the words were not from God, how could we be sure the thoughts were from God? Very slight changes in words or grammar cause dramatic changes in the thought of a sentence.

3. Some of the writers themselves did not understand what they were writing (see Dan 7:15-16; 12:8-9). How could the human writers put God's thoughts into their own words if they did not understand what they were writing? The only solution to this is that God had to dictate to them every word and they simply wrote them down accordingly.

IV. PROOFS OF INSPIRATION

A. The Bible Itself

1. Some would argue that it is circular reasoning to use the Bible's claim as a proof of its inspiration. They say that any book could make such a claim. But the fact is that very few other books have claimed to be written by God Himself. And those which have made such a claim either did not stand the test of time or are of obviously inferior quality (contains historical inaccuracies and inconsistencies).

2. There are many powerful statements of inspiration in the Scriptures (see 2 Tim 3:16; 2 Pet 1:21; 2 Sam 23:2; Ezra 1:1; etc). The phrase "*Thus saith the Lord*" and similar phrases are found over 3,800 times in the Old Testament.

3. Christ placed His stamp of approval on the Scriptures (see Matt 4:4).

B. Indestructibility

1. The Roman emperor Diocletian (AD 245 – 313) decreed in AD 303 that every Bible should be destroyed. He had been told that if he could destroy the Bible he would destroy Christianity because 'Christians are a people of the Book.' Feeling he had succeeded, Diocletian raised a column with the inscription in Latin saying, 'the name of Christian is extinguished.' In AD 312, Constantine succeeded him and replaced all the pagan symbols with the symbol of the cross. This remarkable change took place in less than ten years.

2. Fourteen hundred years after Constantine, the French atheist Voltaire (1694 – 1778) boasted, 'One hundred years from my day there will not be a Bible in the earth except one that is looked upon by an antiquarian (one who study into relics of the past) curiosity seeker.' Just twenty years after the death of Voltaire, the Geneva Bible Society purchased his house for printing the Bible. It later became the Paris headquarters for the British and Foreign Bible Society, which stored and distributed Bibles throughout Europe. "*The grass withereth, the flower fadeth: but the word of our God shall stand for ever*" (Isa 40:8).

3. The indestructibility of the Bible was promised (see Isa 55:11; 59:21; Matt 5:18; 24:35; Luke 16:17; etc).

4. The indestructibility of the Bible was fulfilled in the copying of the manuscripts. Almost as soon as the original manuscripts (Autographs) were written, copies began to be made. Just as a well-loved and used copy of the Bible soon begins to deteriorate, so the original manuscripts did not last long because of constant handling. But God preserved His Word by the hands of dedicated copyists. These men had such a high regard for Scripture that they went to great lengths to ensure the accuracy of their copies. Minute regulations were laid down in the Talmud for their preparation. 'A synagogue roll must be written on the skins of clean animals, prepared for the particular use of the synagogue by a Jew. These must be fastened together with strings taken from clean animals. Every skin must contain a certain number of columns, equal throughout the entire codex (manuscript). The length of each column must not extend over less than forty-eight, or more than sixty lines; and the breadth must consist of thirty letters. The whole copy must be first lined; and if three words be written in it without a line, it is worthless. The ink should be black, neither red, green, nor any colour, and be prepared according to a definite receipt (receipe). An authentic copy must be the exemplar, from which the transcriber ought not in the least to deviate. No word or letter, not even a yod, must be written from memory, the scribe not having looked at the codex before him... Between every consonant the space of a hair or thread must intervene; between every word the breadth of a narrow consonant; between every new parshiah, or section, the breadth of nine consonants; between every book, three lines. The fifth book of Moses must terminate exactly with a line; but the rest need not do so. Besides this, the copyist must sit in Jewish dress, wash his whole body, not begin to write the name of God with a pen newly dipped in ink, and should a king address him while writing that name he must take no notice of him... The rolls in which these regulations are not observed are condemned to be buried in the ground or burn; or they are banished to the schools, to be used as reading-books.

Besides recording varieties of reading, traditions, or conjecture, the Masoretes (Old Testament copyists) undertook a number of calculations which do not enter into the ordinary sphere of texture criticism. They numbered the verses, words, and letters of every book. They calculated the middle word and the middle letter of each. They enumerated verses which contained all the letters of the alphabet, or a certain number of them; and so on. These trivialities, as we may rightly consider them, had yet the effect of securing minute attention to the precise transmission of the text; and they are but an excessive manifestation of a respect for the sacred Scriptures which itself deserves nothing but praise. <u>The Masoretes were indeed anxious that not one jot nor tittle – not one smallest letter nor one tiny part of a letter – of the Law should pass away or be lost'</u> – Sir Frederick Kenyon, *Our Bible and the Ancient Manuscripts* (New York: Harper and Brothers, 1940), pp 38-43.

C. Inerrancy

1. Inerrancy means the Bible is without error throughout, whether it is speaking historically, scientifically or morally. An inerrant Book indicates a perfect Author. Inaccurate writings or speeches would reveal a less-than-perfect author. Deut 18:21-22, *"How shall we know the word which the LORD hath not spoken? When a prophet speaketh in the name of the LORD, if the thing follow not, nor come to pass, that is the thing which the LORD hath not spoken."*

2. Christ authenticated the passages which have most often been challenged as to their accuracy.

Matt. 12:40	Jonah and the whale
Matt. 12:41	Repentance of Nineveh
Luke 17:26-27	The Flood
Luke 17:28-29	Destruction of Sodom
Luke 17:32	Lot's wife turn into a pillar of salt
Luke 4:27	Miraculous healing of Naaman's leprosy
John 3:14	The brazen serpent

3. Those who most often question the accuracy of the Bible are those who do not give it serious study. 'The Bible got mistakes' is an expression usually repeated by an individual ignorant of Biblical truth and has an extremely low view on the Bible.

D. Fulfilled Prophecy

1. Here is a partial listing of Old Testament prophecies that have already been fulfilled in the New Testament.

PROPHECY OF THE PROMISED MESSIAH	OT REFERENCE	NT FULFILLMENT
His Virgin birth	Isa 7:14	Matt 1:20; Lk 1:30-35
Birthplace in Bethlehem	Mic 5:2	Lk 2:4-7

His forerunner, John the Baptist	Isa 40:3	Jn 1:6-8, 19-23
His Triumphal Entry	Zech 9:9-10	Jn 12:12-19
His side pierced at Calvary	Zech 12:10	Jn 19:34
His cry, "My God, My God, why hast Thou forsaken Me?"	Ps 22:1	Matt 27:46
Darkness at His crucifixion	Ps 22:2	Matt 27:45
Mocking at His crucifixion	Ps 22:6-8	Matt 27:39-43
His Hands and feet pierced	Ps 22:16	Jn 20:24-29
Casting lots for His vesture	Ps 22:18	Matt 27:35
His unbroken bones	Ps 34:20	Jn 19:36
Given vinegar to drink	Ps 69:21	Matt 27:34, 48
Buried in a rich man's grave near the wicked	Isa 53:9	Matt 27:57-60
Christ's Resurrection	Ps 16:10; Hos 6:2	Lk 24:1-7
Christ's Ascension	Ps 110:1; Ps 24:3-10	Acts 1:8-11

2. There are many Old Testament prophecies concerning Christ's first coming.

3. Many New Testament prophecies are fulfilled by historical events. The followings are two examples:

a. The destruction of Jerusalem in AD 70. Jesus prophesied in Matt 24:2, "... *there shall not be left here one stone upon another...*" The Roman armies under Titus besieged Jerusalem for 143 days. Josephus records that Titus finally ordered the entire city to be burned to the ground. The city wall 'was so completely leveled with the ground that there was no longer anything to lead those who visited the spot to believe that it had ever been inhabited.'

b. The unnatural death of Simon Peter prophesied by Jesus Christ. Jesus says in John 21:18-19, "Verily, verily, I say unto thee,... when thou shalt be old, thou shalt stretch forth thy hands, and another shall gird thee, and carry thee whither thou wouldest not. This spake he, signifying by what death he should glorify God." Jerome states that Simon Peter (at his request) was crucified upside down. Peter felt he was unworthy to be crucified in the same manner as his Master.

E. Scientific Accuracy

Although the Bible was not written as a science book, yet when the Bible speaks concerning matters of science, it is scientifically accurate. The followings are some examples:

1. God created the universe ex nihilo (out of nothing) – Heb 11:3
2. Moisture in the atmosphere goes through a cycle of evaporation and condensation – Ps 135:7
3. The earth is spherical in shape – Isa 40:22
4. The earth rotates upon its axis – Job 38:13-14
5. The earth is suspended in space – Job 26:7
6. The stars cannot be numbered – Jer 33:22
7. The stars travel in certain paths – Jud 5:20
8. The stars differ in magnitude – 1 Cor 15:41
9. The blood sustains life – Lev 17:11
10. The chemical composition of man and earth is identical – Ps 103:14

F. Historical Accuracy

1. Archaeology has confirmed the existence of peoples who were once questioned by Bible skeptics (eg. The Hittites).

2. Archaeology has confirmed the accuracy of the names, times and places of reign of over forty different kings by means of documents contemporary with the Bible (Belshazzar as king of Babylon).

3. Archaeology has confirmed that writing was highly developed when Moses wrote Pentateuch (the uncovering of Sinai script revealed invention of alphabet well before 1500 BC).

V. INSPIRATION & PRESERVATION

A. Inspiration and Preservation are Twin Doctrines of the Bible!

1. Non-VPPists or anti-VPPists do not believe the God who perfectly inspired His Word has also perfectly preserved His Word. They affirm Verbal Plenary Inspiration (VPI) but deny Verbal Plenary Preservation (VPP). They believe strongly that we do not have an infallible and inerrant Bible TODAY and thereby their denial of the doctrine of VPP. By denying VPP, they might as well deny VPI, for what is the use of an infallible and inerrant Bible in the past but not today?

2. Dr Ian Paisley was absolutely correct to say, "The verbal Inspiration of the Scriptures demands the verbal Preservation of the Scriptures. Those who would deny the need for verbal Preservation cannot be accepted as committed to verbal Inspiration. If there is no preserved Word of God today then the work of Divine Revelation and Divine Inspiration has perished" (*My Plea for the Old Sword*, 103).

3. Dr Timothy Tow, founding pastor of the Bible-Presbyterian Church in Singapore and principal of the Far Eastern Bible College, likewise wrote, "We believe the preservation of Holy Scripture and its Divine inspiration stand in the same position as providence and creation. If Deism teaches a Creator who goes to sleep after creating the world is absurd, to hold to the doctrine of inspiration without preservation is equally illogical. ... Without preservation, all the inspiration, God-breathing into the Scriptures, would be lost. But we have a Bible so pure and powerful in every word and it is so because God has preserved it down through the ages" (*A Theology for Every Christian: Knowing God and His Word*, 47).

4. Dr Hills wrote, "If the doctrine of *divine inspiration* of the Old and New Testament Scriptures is a true doctrine, the doctrine of the *providential preservation* of these Scriptures must also be a true doctrine. It must be that down through the centuries God has exercised a special, providential control over the copying of the Scriptures and the preservation and use of the original text have been available to God's people in every age. God must have done this, for if He gave the Scriptures to His Church by inspiration as the perfect and final revelation of His will, then it is obvious that He would not allow this revelation to disappear or undergo any alteration of its fundamental character" (*The King James Version* Defended, 2).

B. Without Preservation, Inspiration is Meaningless!

1. If we reject the perfect preservation of the Bible today, then we concede that we do not have the inspired Word of God intact, as the words of the originals are not kept pure which the Westminster Divines believed otherwise in their Confession.

2. For centuries, the Church has been upholding and still standing firm on the doctrine of Verbal Plenary Inspiration because without it the Church will surely fall. Inspiration of God's Word can only stand as long as Preservation of the same Word continues to be found in our hand today. Otherwise, what's the point of believing inspiration of the

Scripture? We believe it exactly because God has preserved for us providentially all of His inspired Word today.

(Appendix 2 is the crossword puzzle. Fill in all the answers in the boxes and discover for yourself the twin doctrine of the Holy Scriptures)

VI. SUMMARY

Although the Preservation of God's Word was not taught till this century, it does not mean it is a new teaching. It is as old as the Bible. God's Word declared it, Jesus Himself affirmed it, let us believed it. To deem preservation of God's Word as a new teaching and insist it is a new path is an indirect attack on God and His character. Jesus is the same yesterday, today and forever (Heb 13:8). Is not His Word the same yesterday, today, and forever? Will you tell me God has changed His mind and therefore His Word is not the same today as yesterday?

Let us remember that Satan is still the master of all deception and falsehood. He continues to undermine God's Word since in the Garden of Eden against Adam and Eve. Today his cunning method used is remarkably a 'fool-proof' plan that has turned conservative fundamentalists unknowingly to his side and attack God's providential preservation of His inspired Word. But God's Word stands unwavering, *"for we can do nothing against the truth but for the truth"* (2 Cor 13:8). Amen.

> "False doctrine does not meet men face to face, and proclaim that it is false. It does not blow a trumpet before it, and endeavour openly to turn us away from the truth as it is in Jesus. It does not come before men in broad daylight and summon them to surrender. It approaches us secretly, quietly, insidiously, plausibly, and in such a way as to disarm man's suspicion, and throw him off his guard. It is the wolf in sheep's clothing, and Satan in the garb of an angel of light, who have always proved the most dangerous foes of the Church" (J C Ryle, *Warnings to the Churches*, 56).

Lesson 2: Appendix 1

WRITER	INSPIRED WRITINGS
Moses	Genesis, Exodus, Leviticus, Numbers, Deuteronomy, Psalm 90
Joshua	Joshua
Ezra	Ezra, 1 & 2 Chronicles (probably; not certain)
Nehemiah	Nehemiah
Mordecai	Esther (?) Ezra and Nehemiah are also possible writers of Esther)
David	Psalms (wrote at least 73 of the Psalms)
Asaph	Psalm 50, Psalms 73 – 83
Descendents of Korah	Psalms 42, 44 – 49, 84, 87 – 88
Heman the Ezrahite	Psalm 88
Ethan the Ezrahite	Psalm 89
Solomon	Proverbs, Ecclesiastes, Song of Solomon, Psalm 72 (?), Psalm 127
Isaiah	Isaiah
Jeremiah	Jeremiah
Ezekiel	Ezekiel
Daniel	Daniel
Hosea	Hosea
Joel	Joel
Amos	Amos
Obadiah	Obadiah
Jonah	Jonah
Micah	Micah
Habakkuk	Habakkuk
Zephaniah	Zephaniah
Haggai	Haggai
Zechariah	Zechariah
Malachi	Malachi

Matthew	Gospel of Matthew
Mark	Gospel of Mark
Luke	Gospel of Luke, Acts of the Apostles
John the Apostle	Gospel of John, 1,2,3 John, Revelation
Paul	Romans, 1,2 Corinthians, Galatians, Ephesians, Philippians, Colossians, 1,2 Thessalonians, 1,2 Timothy, Titus, Philemon, Hebrews (?)
James	James
Peter	1,2 Peter
Jude	Jude

Lesson 2: Appendix 2

Twin Doctrines of Holy Scripture

			1	B						
2	E						L			
	3	V								
4									E	
		5	F							
			6					H		
			7	A						
							N	8		
			9	S						
		10							S	
11	D									

1. Another word for the Word of God.
2. God's Word is _____ means it stands for ever and ever.
3. Today, there are many modern English _____ of the Bible.
4. "All _____ is given by inspiration of God ..." (2 Timothy 3:16).
5. "So then _____ cometh by hearing, and hearing by the Word of God

(Romans 10:17).
6. "And ye shall know the _____, and the _____ shall make you free" (John 8:32).
7. Westminster Divines has affirmed God's Word to have "kept pure in all _____..."
8. God's Word reveals God's complete plan of _____ for sinful men through Jesus Christ.
9. _____ has separated man from God, and has caused man to rebel against His Word.
10. In the Old Testament, the _____ spoke God's message to His people.
11. Though the Bible is written by 40 different men, the intent is not human but _____.

Twin Doctrines of Holy Scripture

			1	P							
								G	2		
		3	H								
	4			S							
5	R										
	6		..		S						
	7	L									
	8		W								
9	F										
	10							L			
	11	D									
12										N	

1. "The words of the LORD are _____ words: as silver tried in a furnace of earth, purified seven times" (Psalm 12:6).
2. "The law of the LORD is perfect, _____ the soul ..." (Psalm 19:7).
3. The Bible is written in the languages of _____, Aramaic and Greek.
4. "Heaven and earth shall _____ away, but my words shall not _____ away" (Matthew 24:35).
5. Another name for the Greek New Testament Received Text is Textus _____.
6. "He that is of God heareth God's _____ " (John 8:47).
7. "Jesus ... said ..., If a man _____ me, he will keep my words..." (John 14:23).
8. "The _____ of the LORD is perfect..." (Psalm 19:7).
9. The KJB is the most _____ translation of the original languages of the Holy Scriptures.
10. We do not have the _____ manuscripts of the Holy Scriptures today.
11. "For the time will come when they will not endure sound _____..." (2 Tim 4:3).
12. No Bible _____ is 100% equivalent to the inspired Hebrew, Aramaic and Greek Scriptures.

LESSON 3

BIBLICAL SUPPORT I

For The Doctrine of Verbal Plenary Preservation

(TO BE CONTINUED IN THE NEXT LESSON 4)

I. REVIEW

A. Meaning of Verbal Plenary Preservation

Verbal" = words

"Plenary" = total, complete, 100%, all (to the minutest jot and tittle)

"Preservation" = kept free from corruption, safeguarded

B. What "Words"?

The "Words" of God that are being preserved by God refer to the words in the original languages that were inspired by God (2 Tim 3:16, 2 Pet 1:21)

The "Words" are the Hebrew and Greek words that God took upon Himself not just to inspire holy men of God to write down but also to preserve.

II. THE BASIS OF THE DOCTRINE OF VPP

Read 2 Timothy 3:1-2, 7-9, 13-17.

This passage warns us that as we live in these last days, we are living in perilous times (2 Tim 3:1), i.e. DANGEROUS times.

One of the many dangers the Church faces in these last days is that men (pastors, church leaders included) "shall be lovers of their own selves, covetous, boasters, proud, blasphemers, disobedient to parents, unthankful, unholy…,ever learning, and never able to come to the knowledge of the truth…evil men and seducers shall wax worse and worse, deceiving, and being deceived." (2 Tim 3:2, 7, 13).

Before we point our fingers at others, let us first check ourselves that we DO NOT fall into this category. Let us examine ourselves honestly before our omniscient God. "If we confess our sins, he is faithful and just to forgive us [our] sins, and to cleanse us from all unrighteousness." (1 John 1:9)

While Paul warns Timothy of the dangers, he also gave Timothy the shield against these dangerous men in 2 Tim 3:14-15: "continue thou in the things which thou hast learned and hast been assured of, knowing of whom thou hast learned [them]. And that from a child thou hast known the holy scriptures, which are able to make thee wise unto salvation through faith which is in Christ Jesus."

The shield against them is the SCRIPTURE, the Word of God, the Bible.

The scripture made Timothy "wise unto salvation through faith" (v 15), that is the Bible gave Timothy the good news of salvation and Timothy was saved. BUT, he is not to throw out the scripture once he is saved.

Paul instructed Timothy to "continue thou in the things which thou hast learned" (v 14), that is Timothy is to continue to know the Word of God and be guided by the Word of God. In other words, the Bible is given to us NOT only to show us the way to heaven.

Paul goes on to describe scripture and what it is given to us for.

"All scripture [is] given by inspiration of God, and [is] profitable for DOCTRINE, for REPROOF, for CORRECTION, for INSTRUCTION in righteousness: That the man of God may be perfect, throughly furnished unto all good works." (2 Tim 3:16-17)

That is, God's Word is given to:

- let us know God's teachings

-- admonish us when we have failed to do right

-- correct us when we have done wrong

-- instruct/direct us in the right path to take.

And all these are for the purpose that the believer (having received salvation) will grow/ mature in his faith and be equipped to serve God, to live for God.

So, be very careful about people who say: "We are all going to end up in heaven, and that is enough. Never mind about the other teachings in the Bible."

Brethren, it is not enough that we are all heading for heaven. Yes, scripture shows us the way to heaven, BUT scripture is given also to show us WHAT God wants to us to know and HOW we are to live on earth while we are on the way to heaven and that we are to GROW in maturity.

"All scripture [is]... profitable for DOCTRINE...." So, what does scripture say about the Doctrine of the PRESERVATION of the inspired Word of God?

III. AN OVERVIEW OF THE BIBLE'S TEACHING ON VPP

A. The Bible teaches the Doctrine of Preservation

Psalm 12:6–7 The words of the LORD [are] pure words: [as] silver tried in a furnace of earth, purified seven times. Thou shalt keep them, O LORD, thou shalt preserve them from this generation for ever.

Psalm 33:11 The counsel of the LORD standeth for ever, the thoughts of his heart to all generations.

Psalm 78:1–7 Give ear, O my people, [to] my law: incline your ears to the words of my mouth. I will open my mouth in a parable: I will utter dark sayings of old: Which we have heard and known, and our fathers have told us. We will not hide [them] from their children, shewing to the generation to come the praises of the LORD, and his strength, and his wonderful works that he hath done. For he established a testimony in

Jacob, and appointed a law in Israel, which he commanded our fathers, that they should make them known to their children: That the generation to come might know [them, even] the children [which] should be born; [who] should arise and declare [them] to their children: That they might set their hope in God, and not forget the works of God, but keep his commandments.

Psalm 100:5 For the LORD [is] good; his mercy [is] everlasting; and his truth [endureth] to all generations.

Psalm 105:8 He hath remembered his covenant for ever, the word [which] he commanded to a thousand generations.

Psalm 111:7–8 The works of his hands [are] verity and judgment; all his commandments [are] sure. They stand fast for ever and ever, [and are] done in truth and uprightness.

Psalm 117:2 For his merciful kindness is great toward us: and the truth of the LORD [endureth] for ever. Praise ye the LORD.

Psalm 119:89 For ever, O LORD, thy word is settled in heaven.

Psalm 119:152 Concerning thy testimonies, I have known of old that thou hast founded them for ever.

Psalm 119:160 Thy word [is] true [from] the beginning: and every one of thy righteous judgments [endureth] for ever.

Isaiah 40:8 The grass withereth, the flower fadeth: but the word of our God shall stand for ever.

Isaiah 59:21 As for me, this [is] my covenant with them, saith the LORD; My spirit that [is] upon thee, and my words which I have put in thy mouth, shall not depart out of thy mouth, nor out of the mouth of thy seed, nor out of the mouth of thy seed's seed, saith the LORD, from henceforth and for ever.

Matthew 4:4 But he answered and said, It is written, Man shall not live by bread alone, but by every word that proceedeth out of the mouth of God.

Matthew 5:17–18 Think not that I am come to destroy the law, or the prophets: I am not come to destroy, but to fulfil. For verily I say unto

*you, Till heaven and earth pass, one jot or one tittle shall <u>in no wise</u>
<u>pass</u> from the law, till all be fulfilled.*

*Matthew 24:35 Heaven and earth shall pass away, but my words <u>shall</u>
<u>not pass away</u>.*

*John 10:35 If he called them gods, unto whom the word of God came,
and the scripture <u>cannot be broken</u>;*

*1 Peter 1:23–25 Being born again, not of corruptible seed, but of
incorruptible, by the word of God, which <u>liveth and abideth for ever</u>. For
all flesh [is] as grass, and all the glory of man as the flower of grass.
The grass withereth, and the flower thereof falleth away: But the word
of the Lord <u>endureth for ever</u>. And this is the word which by the gospel
is preached unto you.*

<u>B. The Bible teaches the preservation of all the Words (not just
doctrines) of God</u>

*Psalm 12:6–7 <u>The words</u> of the LORD [are] pure words: [as] silver tried
in a furnace of earth, purified seven times. <u>Thou shalt keep them</u>, O
LORD, <u>thou shalt preserve them</u> from this generation for ever.*

Psalm 119:89 For ever, O LORD, <u>thy word is settled</u> in heaven.

*Isaiah 40:8 The grass withereth, the flower fadeth: but <u>the word</u> of our
God <u>shall stand for ever</u>.*

*Matthew 4:4 But he answered and said, It is written, Man shall not live
by bread alone, but by <u>every word</u> that proceedeth out of the mouth of
God.*

*Matthew 5:17–18 Think not that I am come to destroy the law, or the
prophets: I am not come to destroy, but to fulfil. For verily I say unto
you, Till heaven and earth pass, <u>one jot or one tittle</u> shall in no wise
pass from the law, till all be fulfilled.*

*Matthew 24:35 Heaven and earth shall pass away, but <u>my words</u> shall
not pass away.*

*1 Peter 1:24–25 For all flesh [is] as grass, and all the glory of man as
the flower of grass. The grass withereth, and the flower thereof falleth*

away: But <u>the word</u> of the Lord endureth for ever. And this is <u>the word</u> which by the gospel is preached unto you.

<u>C. The Bible reveals that the purpose of the Verbal Plenary Preservation of God's Words is to sanctify God's children when they obey His Word</u>

Deuteronomy 4:2 Ye shall not add unto the word which I command you, neither shall ye diminish [ought] from it, that ye may keep the commandments of the LORD your God which I command you.

Deuteronomy 29:29 The secret [things belong] unto the LORD our God: but those [things which are] revealed [belong] unto us and to our children for ever, that [we] may do all the words of this law.

Joshua 1:8 This book of the law shall <u>not depart out of thy mouth</u>; but thou shalt <u>meditate therein</u> day and night, that thou mayest <u>observe to do</u> according to all that is written therein: for then thou shalt make thy way prosperous, and then thou shalt have good success.

Psalm 78:1–7 Give ear, O my people, [to] my law: incline your ears to the words of my mouth. I will open my mouth in a parable: I will utter dark sayings of old: Which we have heard and known, and our fathers have told us. We will not hide [them] from their children, shewing to the generation to come the praises of the LORD, and his strength, and his wonderful works that he hath done. For he established a testimony in Jacob, and appointed a law in Israel, which he commanded our fathers, that they should make them known to their children: That the generation to come <u>might know [them</u>, even] the children [which] should be born; [who] should arise and declare [them] to their children: That they <u>might set their hope in God, and not forget the works of God, but keep his commandments</u>.

Proverbs 5:7 Hear me now therefore, O ye children, and <u>depart not from the words</u> of my mouth.

Matthew 4:4 But he answered and said, It is written, Man shall <u>not live by bread alone, but by every word</u> that proceedeth out of the mouth of God.

John 20:30–31 And many other signs truly did Jesus in the presence of his disciples, which are not written in this book: But these are written, that *ye might believe* that Jesus is the Christ, the Son of God; and that believing ye might have life through his name.

Romans 10:17 So then *faith [cometh]* by hearing, and hearing by the word of God.

John 17:17 *Sanctify* them through thy truth: thy word is truth.

2 Timothy 3:16–17 All scripture [is] given by inspiration of God, and [is] *profitable for doctrine, for reproof, for correction, for instruction* in righteousness: That the man of God *may be perfect*, throughly furnished unto all *good works*.

Revelation 22:7 Behold, I come quickly: blessed [is] he that *keepeth* the sayings of the prophecy of this book.

IV. OUR STARTING POINT

Want to know whether the doctrine of the 100% preservation of the God-breathed Hebrew and Greek words is true or false? Check it out in the Bible. We will never go wrong when we look first to the Word of God. And the Bible teaches that God Himself will ensure the preservation of His own inspired words as we saw above.

THE WAY THAT PLEASES GOD	THE WAY THAT DISPLEASES GOD
Start with: What the Bible says	Start with: What men/scholars say
God's wisdom	Man's wisdom
Faith	Facts
	("subjective interpretation")

Inspiration	Inspiration
Preservation	Deny Preservation
	(Preserved with mistakes/No preservation/Ltd preservation/Only autographs are preserved but don't have it today)
Inerrant Bible	Errant Bible
Infallible Bible	Fallible Bible
End with: Perfect Bible today	End with: Imperfect Bible today

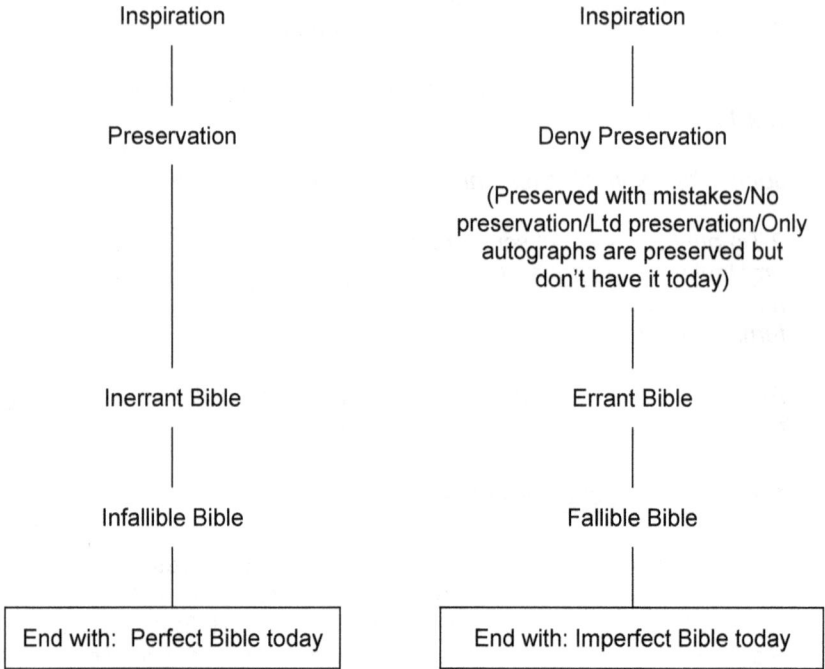

V. CONCLUSION: OUR RESPONSE

The Bible is certainly NOT silent about the verbal, plenary preservation of God's Word. And therefore we must by faith believe what it says.

Read Luke 1:34-38.

Let us respond with the faith of Mary (Lk 1:38) and say *"Be it according to Your Word, O Lord."*

Hebrews 11:6: "But without faith [it is] impossible to please [him]: for he that cometh to God must believe that he is, and [that] he is a rewarder of them that diligently seek him."

With God nothing is impossible. If God says He will preserve His words, He is ABLE to keep His promise and He WILL preserve His words.

Pray for faith to believe.

Application Question:

How will you respond to those who attack the Verbal Plenary Preservation of God's Word by saying "VPP is a new teaching" or "VPP is a theory" ?

"The devil and his agents have been blowing at Scripture light, but could never blow it out; a clear sign that it was lighted from heaven....The letter of Scripture has been preserved, without any corruption, in the original tongue." [1]

---

[1] Thomas Watson, "A Body of Divinity" (Edinburgh: The Banner of Truth Trust, 1965, First published in 1692), 27.

LESSON 4

BIBLICAL SUPPORT II

For The Doctrine of Verbal Plenary Preservation

(TO BE CONTINUED IN THE NEXT LESSON 5)

Psalm 12:6-7 and Psalm 19:7-10

I. INTRODUCTION

The unending attacks on the Word of God know no bound. God's people must be vigilant and sober for the day of deliverance is nearer than we think. To let our guard down would signify the spiritual death of our present and future generations.

When the doctrine of inspiration came under attack the defenders of the Word of God in times past had only one clear-cut verse to support the doctrine. It was 2 Timothy 3:16. They fought tooth and nail defending this truth amidst all the distortions and misinterpretations.

Finally the battle was over and the line was clearly drawn. On the one side there were the fundamentalists who held on to the doctrine of inspiration as stated in our church Constitution which is our heritage. On the other side were the modernists and neo-evangelicals who believe in limited inerrancy and infallibility where inspiration was only in spiritual matters or matters that pertain to man's salvation. Anything else would have mistakes, which they called minor ones.

Today we thank God that we have more than one verse from God's Word defending the doctrine of preservation. Even though there are many verses that teach preservation, the same attack that was used to undermine the doctrine of inspiration is also employed today. Re-interpretation or misinterpretation of Bible verses is also used.

II. INTERPRETING PSALM 12:6-7—Perfect Word of God preserved

Psalm 12:6-7: "*The words of the LORD are pure words: as silver tried in a furnace of earth, purified seven times. Thou shalt keep them, O LORD, thou shalt preserve them from this generation for ever.*"

The teaching from these two verses appears quite clear that God would preserve His Holy Word for ever. Yet many have argued otherwise. They say that the preservation in verse 7 refers to people only.

A. Grammar and Syntax arguments

1. Those who interpret Psalm 12:7 as referring to people and not the Word of God say that since the pronominal suffix "keep them" in verse 7a is in the masculine gender (plural) and "the words of the LORD" in verse 6 is in the feminine gender (plural), "them" must refer to "people." In order for it to refer to God's Word the pronominal suffix must also be in the feminine gender like the substantive. This is a faulty reasoning based upon a wrong assumption. As Gesenius, a classic Hebrew grammarian teaches, "Through a weakening in the distinction of gender, which is noticeable elsewhere. And which probably passed from the colloquial language into that of literature, masculine suffixes (especially in the plural) are not infrequently used to refer to feminine substantives." **[Gesenius' Hebrew Grammar**, edited and enlarged by E. Kitsch, second edition by A. E. Cowley, (Oxford: Clarendon Press, 1910, 2nd edition), page 440, Section O].

Some examples from the OT where this phenomenon occurs include:

Genesis 31:9, "Thus God hath taken away the cattle of your **[masculine plural pronoun suffix --** referring to Rachel and Leah) father, and given them to me."

Genesis 32:15, "Thirty milch camels with their **[masculine plural pronoun suffix -** referring to the thirty female camels) colts, forty kine, and ten bulls, twenty she asses, and ten foals."

Exodus 1:21, "And it came to pass, because the midwives feared God, that he made them **[masculine plural pronoun suffix --** a reference to the midwives] houses.

Psalm 119:111, "Thy testimonies **[feminine plural noun]** have I taken as an heritage for ever: for they **[masculine plural pronoun]** are the rejoicing of my heart."

Psalm 119:129, "Thy testimonies **[feminine plural noun]** are wonderful: therefore doth my soul keep them **[masculine plural pronoun suffix]**."

Psalm 119:152, "Concerning thy testimonies **[feminine plural noun]**, I have known of old that thou hast founded them **[masculine plural pronoun suffix]** for ever."

Psalm 119:167, "My soul hath kept thy testimonies **[feminine plural noun]**; and I love them **[masculine plural noun suffix]** exceedingly."

These are only a few examples cited to demonstrate the nature of feminine plural nouns in relation to their masculine pronouns. According to the Hebrew language, it is most legitimate to refer the suffix pronoun "them **-- masculine plural pronominal suffix** (verse 7a)" to "the words **-- feminine plural substantive** of the LORD (verse 6)." For them to insist that the gender must be the same is eisegesis. We cannot force the Word of God to say what we want it to say. Also it is wrong to insist that biblical Hebrew grammar and syntax must conform to the English grammar and syntax.

Thomas Strouse agrees and wrote, "…it is not uncommon, especially in the Psalter, for feminine plural noun synonyms for the 'words' of the Lord to be the antecedent for masculine plural pronouns/pronominal suffixes, which seem to 'masculinize' the verbal extension of the patriarchal God of the Old Testament. …As the KJB/TR bibliologists have argued all along, both the context and the grammar (proximity rule and accepted gender discordance) of Psalm 12:6-7 demand the teaching of the preservation of the Lord's pure words for every generation." [http://www.wayoflife.org/fbns/strouse-psalm127.html]

2. Another argument they cited is that the pronominal suffix "preserve them (verse 7b)" is in the singular and KJB translators have no right to change it to "them (plural)." It is true that the pronominal suffix for "preserve them" in verse 7b is a third person masculine singular suffix (him).

Why did the KJB translators translate it as "them"?

The key is that in the addition of the suffix, the Holy Spirit wanted to emphasize the verb "preserve" so that an "energetic nun" (the letter "n") is added before attaching the pronominal suffix. When this occurs an additional rule comes into operation in the Hebrew language. **There is no masculine plural pronominal suffix in the third person when the energetic nun is applied to a verb.** [See **Gesenius**, page 157-158 Section 4, I]. Hence the Scripture writer, through the inspiration of the Holy Spirit, used the singular masculine pronominal suffix, retaining the same gender as in "keep them (verse 7a)."

Therefore it is very legitimate and consistent with Hebrew grammar for the KJB translators to translate the masculine singular pronoun suffix with the energetic nun as a masculine plural pronoun -- "them."

B. Contextual argument

When we speak of context, it is the immediate context that is considered first, and not the distant context. The immediate context is of course the Words of the LORD. Hence the preservation and keeping (guarding) would be the Words of the LORD. We know that the syntax and grammar allow it.

Verse 6 is what is known as an emblematic parallelism where the purity of God's Word is likened to the sevenfold purification (as pure as you can ever get) process of purifying silver where every bit of dross is burned away leaving behind the purest silver [Tremper Longman III, **How to Read the Psalms**, (Downers Grove: InterVarsity Press, 1988), 100]. This verse teaches that the Words of the LORD are without error or fallibility and it is 100% perfect.

Verse 7 is known as a synonymous parallelism where the second line restates what is mentioned in the first, but using different words (Longman III, 99). As mentioned before, the use of the energetic "nun" emphasizes the act of preservation. This preservation is forever.

The relationship between verses 6 and 7 is what we call synthetic parallelism where the second verse adds or expands on the teaching mentioned in the first verse. These two verses combined together teach that the Words of God which are perfect like silver purified seven times will be preserved by God forever!

The contrast within the entire psalm would be the words of these evil men pitted against the Words of the LORD. These evil men speak vanity and flattery (verse 2) and boast that their words will prevail and no one is lord over them (verse 4). The Words of the LORD counter that it is the Lord's Word that will prevail over the words of the evil ones.

This is the assurance and comfort that the LORD gives to His people. Do not fear the words of these evil flatterers and boasters; trust in the Words of the LORD that is purified seven times as opposed to the words of the evil men which are vain, proud and stem from a double heart (verse 2). God will keep (guard) His Holy Words and preserve (action is emphasized by the energetic nun) them from this generation forever. The LORD gave this verbal assurance to that generation and after because He knew they needed it. God's people were plagued by the many wicked words that came from evil men to confuse and confound them.

The faith of the believers was put to the test, they had to choose to believe and trust in the inerrant, infallible and divinely inspired Word of God Almighty or the errant, fallible words of sinful men. The same decision is asked of every Christian today on the issue of the doctrine of preservation of God's Holy, inerrant, infallible Word.

It must not be intimated that from before this time, God did not preserve His Holy Word. This is faulty hermeneutics. Argument from silence is very dangerous and can lead to all kinds of wrong doctrine. For example, Ephesians 1:4 teaches us that the believers' salvation have been chosen in Him [Christ] before the foundation of the world. Does it mean that the believers in the Old Testament were not chosen before the foundation of the world? Of course we cannot arrive at this erroneous conclusion. Progressive revelation teaches that it took more than one thousand five hundred years for the Bible to be given to us completely intact and perfectly [from Moses around 1445 B.C. to the Apostle John who wrote Revelation, the last book of the New Testament, around 95 A.D.]. When a truth is revealed to God's people, it does not mean that this was the "activation" of that truth. It simply points to the fact that this was the first time God has revealed or taught this truth to His people, something which He has been doing all the time. The doctrines of the indwelling of the Holy Spirit, Election, the doctrine of the Trinity, the Trinitarian involvement in the giving of gifts, God giving gifts according to His sovereign will, and every Christian being given at least one gift are some of the doctrines which are found clearly taught in the New Testament but not taught or implied only in the Old Testament. These doctrines are clearly taught in the New Testament.

C. Bible Translations—past and present on Psalm 12:6-7

David Cloud wrote correctly, "The bifurcation of the Reformation Bible tradition and the post-19th century English Bibles is seen in the New Revised Standard Version render[ing of] Psalm 12:7, "You O Lord, will protect us; you will guard us from this generation forever." In a similar manner, the New International Version translates verse 7, "O Lord, you will keep us safe and protect us from such people forever." In spite of Biblia Hebraica Stuttgartensia reading "keep them" and "preserve him," both the NRSV and NIV have elected not to translate the Hebrew and have, in its place, substituted a translation from the Greek and Latin rendering of these two pronouns. By so doing, the editors of these translations have endorsed one exegetical tradition, the Greek-Latin, to the exclusion of the other, the Hebraic, and by doing so have censured any further debate within the Hebrew exegetical tradition itself.

"This essay will show the diversity of the textual and exegetical tradition of Psalm 12:6-7 ... By so doing, the inadequacy of modern renditions of Psalm 12:7 will be exposed...

"*Michael Ayguan (1340-1416)* ... On Psalm 12:7 Ayguan comments, Keep them: that is, not as the passage is generally taken, Keep or guard Thy people, but Thou shalt keep, or make good, Thy words: and by doing so, shalt preserve him--him, the needy, him, the poor--from this generation...

"*Martin Luther's German Bible* ... Following the arrangement of this Psalm, Luther penned a hymn, two stanzas of which reflect his understanding of verse 6 and 7: ... "Thy truth thou wilt preserve, O Lord, from this vile generation..." In poetic form, Luther grasps the significance of this verse both for the preservation of those who are oppressed and for the Word of God. The two-pronged significance of this interpretation to both people and God's words in Luther's Psalter was to have wide-ranging significance in the English Bible tradition.

"*Calvin's Commentary on the Psalms* ... in the body of the commentary he writes, 'Some give this exposition of the passage, Thou wilt keep them, namely, thy words; but this does not seem to me to be suitable."

[Thus while Calvin did not believe Psalm 12:7 referred to the Word of God, he admits that others did hold this view in his day.]

"*Coverdale Bible, 1535* ... reads for [verse 7] of Psalm 12: "Keep them therefore (O Lord) and preserve us from this generation for ever." With the absence of "Thou shalt" to begin verse 7, there is a direct connection between 'words' and 'keep them.' In the first clause, Coverdale intended the words to be kept; in the second clause people are in view..."

"*The Matthew Bible 1537.* ... In Psalm 12:67 Rogers translated, "The words of the Lord are pure words as the silver, which from the earth is tried and purified vii times in the fire. Keep them therefore (O Lord) and preserve us from this generation for ever." Following Coverdale, Rogers makes a clear connection in his translation between the words being the antecedent to "them." ... The significance of Roger's marginal note is that two of the greatest Hebrew scholars referred to by the Reformation writers differed on the interpretation of "them" in Psalms 12:7. [Thus we see that the interpretation of this verse was also divided among Jewish scholars.]

"*The Third Part of the Bible, 1550.* Taken from Becke's text of 1549 this edition of the scriptures contains the Psalter, Proverbs, Ecclesiastes and the Song of Songs. ... In verse 7 there is a note at them which states, 'some understand here certain men, some others word." Again, the translators and exegetes allowed breadth of interpretation of "them" to include people and words.

"*The Geneva Bible, 1560.* ... The preface reads, "Then comforting himself and others with the assurance of God's help, he commendeth the constant vigil that God observeth in keeping his promises." The text reads, "The words of the Lord are pure words, as the silver, tried in a furnace of earth, fined seven fold. Thou wilt keep them, O Lord: Thou wilt preserve him from this generation forever." [The margin reads, "Because the Lords word and promise is true and unchangeable, he will perform it and preserve the poor from this wicked generation." Thus the Geneva took a position that verse 7 applies both to the preservation of the Bible and of God's people.]

"*Annotations by Henry Ainsworth,* 1626. Briggs commends Ainsworth as the "prince of Puritan commentators" and that his commentary on the Psalms is a "monument of learning." ... Ainsworth states that "the sayings" [of Psalm 12:7] are "words" or "promises" that are "tried" or "examined" "as in a fire." He cross references the reader to Psalm 18:31; 119:140; and Proverbs 30:5, each reference having to do with the purity of the word.

"*Matthew Poole's 1685 Commentary of the Psalms* ... writes at verse seven, "Thou shalt keep them; either, 1. The poor and needy, ver. 5 ... Or, 2. Thy words or promises last mentioned, ver. 6. ...

"In summary ... [t]he only sure conclusion is that there is no consensus within the English Bible tradition for the interpretation of "them" in Psalm 12:7 and it was precisely this lack of agreement within the tradition which was the genius of the ambiguity of the King James Version's rendering. ... by choosing a Greek-Latin basis the modern versions elect to overlook the Reformation's Hebrew basis for translation in Psalm 12:6-7; and the churchly tradition in the new versions is censored by not including a translation that is broad enough to include both interpretations--oppressed people and God's words" (Peter Van Kleeck, *The Translational and Exegetical Rendering of Psalm 12:7 Primarily Considered in the Churchly Tradition of the 16th and 17th Centuries and Its Expression in the Reformation English Bibles: The Genius of Ambiguity,* March 1993).

[Taken from [http://www.wayoflife.org/fbns/fbns/fbns88.html]

III. INTERPRETING PSALM 19:7-10—Nature of the Word of God explained

A. Psalm 19:7-10:

"The law of the LORD is perfect, converting the soul: the testimony of the LORD is sure, making wise the simple. The statutes of the LORD are right, rejoicing the heart: the commandment of the LORD is pure, enlightening the eyes. The fear of the LORD is clean, enduring for ever: the judgments of the LORD are true and righteous altogether. More to be desired are they than gold, yea, than much fine gold: sweeter also than honey and the honeycomb."

B. Contextual Observations

Psalm 19 teaches God's revelations. Psalm 19:1-6 refers to the general revelation of God through His creation. Psalm 19:7-14 teaches special revelation through God's Holy Word. The Word of God is described by the Psalmist in these six ways: the law, the testimony, the statutes, the commandments, fear and judgments. The nature of the Word of God is described as: perfect, sure, right, pure, clean and true. The effect of the Word of God in the heart and lives of the believer is described as: converting the soul, making wise the simple, rejoicing the heart, enlightening the eyes, enduring for ever and righteous altogether.

The totality of the richness of the Word of God is seen here by the use of these six different nouns. Its infinite value is seen in the description by the Word of God in using "**perfect**" which means "without blemish" i.e. absolutely no mistakes; "**sure**" which means "faithfulness and trust worthy"; "**right**" which means "straight and righteous"; "**pure**" which means "clean and clear and void of impurities"; "**clean**" which means "pure in the moral sense"; and "**true**" which means "trustworthiness or verity i.e. contains no falsehood or errors," to capture the depth and breadth of the Word of God in its totality.

On the meaning of the word "perfect" as used here Barnes wrote, "The meaning is that it lacks nothing in order to its completeness; nothing in order that it might be what it should be. It is complete as a revelation of divine truth; it is complete as a rule of conduct. As explained above, this refers not only to the law of God as the word is commonly employed now, but to the whole of divine truth as revealed. It is absolutely true; it is adapted with consummate wisdom to the wants of man; it is an unerring guide of conduct. There is nothing there which would lead men into error or sin; there is nothing essential for man to know which may not be found there. [**Albert Barnes' Notes on the Bible**, Swordsearcher 4.7]"

That the Word of God was perfect to the Psalmist is an understatement. For the Psalmist to ever think that the Word of God contains the slightest degree of impurity or error or mistake was unthinkable. The highest regard the psalmist gives to the Word of God is clearly seen in the use of the six nouns.

IV. CONCLUSION

The Word of God is the only "catalyst" used by the Spirit of God to transform lives and make children of darkness into children of God's marvelous light, why would God then after more than 1,500 years of inspiration and writing of God's Word not preserve all His words for future generations? We thank God that He did.

Psalm 12:6-7 teaches us that God has preserved His perfect Word perfectly for His people. God inspired His Word perfectly, inerrant, infallible and He also preserved the same Word for His people throughout the ages so that every generation can assuredly say, "Thus saith the LORD!" with absolute confidence.

Psalm 19:7-10 teaches us that the Word of God is more than perfect in all its glory but also purity, verity, surety, righteousness and truthfulness. The Word of God cannot have mistakes and must be perfect at inspiration and perfectly preserved by God Himself throughout the ages for all of God's people. Anything less would be foolishness like a man shooting his own foot! AMEN.

LESSON 5

BIBLICAL SUPPORT III

For The Doctrine of Verbal Plenary Preservation

(TO BE CONTINUED IN THE NEXT LESSON 6)

Psalm 119:89

I. INTRODUCTION

Psalm 119:89 LAMED: "For ever, O LORD, thy word is settled [Niphal participle] in heaven."

This is the beginning of a new section (verses 89-96) in the treatment of the Word of God. This is easily seen in the Hebrew Bible where all the eight verses begin with the letter Lamed (the letter "L" in English).

The focus of this new section on the Word of God is that "the Word of God is forever settled."

II. INTERPRETING PSALM 119:89 – The forever settled Word

A. Meaning of "forever settled"

"Settled" means "to set up" or "to establish". It is in the Niphal stem which makes the verb passive i.e. "to be set up or to be established." As a participle the emphasis would be on the action of the verb.

The qualifier to this verb is the word "forever." The meaning of the two words combined together emphasizes the fact that the Word of God will be established forever.

The word of God will not change. It will not be lost, every part of it. It will be established forever.

B. What is "forever settled"?

What is forever settled is the Word of God, all of it. Although most of the OT and the entire NT were not written yet when Psalm 119 was penned, the truth of this doctrine is by way of application extended to the entire Bible from Genesis to Revelation. All sixty-six books of the Bible are the very Word of God. Therefore the forever established Word of God would definitely include all the books of the Bible.

Barnes Notes have this to add, "The word rendered 'settled' means properly 'to set, to put, to place;' and then, to stand, to cause to stand, to set up, as a column, Gen. 35:20; an altar, Gen. 33:20; a monument, 1 Sam. 15:12. The meaning here is, that the word - the law - the promise - of God was made firm, established, stable, in heaven; and would be so forever and ever. What God had ordained as law would always remain law; what he had affirmed would always remain true; what he had promised would be sure forever." [**Albert Barnes' Notes of the Bible**—SwordSearcher 4.7]

Barnes is correct to make the observation that the law of God will be established forever and it is good that he added "what he had promised would be sure forever." To this it must be added that the phrase used in Psalm 119:89 is "God's Word" which means all the words of God. In other words, the scope of the forever settled word is every jot and tittle without exception.

The Word of God must not be dichotomized into some parts more or some parts less inspired than others, where the parts that are less inspired may have mistakes but that which is more inspired cannot have mistakes. The measure of those parts which are supposed to be "more inspired" are mostly defined as those parts that pertain to "man's salvation."

However, God has never at any time in the Bible teaches different levels of inspiration. Inspiration is absolute and has only one standard. ALL of the words of God are equally inspired, including the numbers, names of places and people. These letters and every word including their tenses, person, gender, and number are all inspired and are inerrant, infallible. They are divinely inspired and preserved.

The dichotomizing of the Word of God into different levels of inspiration and also preservation is a deadly presupposition and teaching. This deadly approach is compounded by the notion that man's salvation becomes the sovereign yardstick of what constitutes as more inspired or more preserved. Such man-centered theology is a ploy of the Devil to inflate man's ego and to deceive man. The whole Bible is always God-centered.

Every word of God is inspired and of equal value in the eyes of God. Man has no right to segmentize God's Word into less important and more important according to his whims and fancies.

C. Forever Settled in Heaven

On earth everything changes. The world continues to decay with every passing year. It is said that the ozone layer has increased in size and the temperature is rising. The second law of thermal dynamics teaches that all matters decay and break down. Multi-billion-dollar companies that used to be the life line of thousands of employees are now bankrupt. All human beings grow old and die. Nations that used to be superpowers are now minions. For example Babylon used to rule a vast empire in the Middle East but now has become a weak nation. Greece was a superpower in the days of Alexander the Great where he thought he had conquered the whole world and there was nothing left for young Alexander to conquer. Today Greece is a small insignificant nation not ranked among the superpowers. Superpowers come and superpowers get replaced! Everything on planet earth is never settled.

But the Word of God is settled in heaven. It means that the Word of God will not be like the ever changing earth, which changes all the time. The Word of God is settled in heaven. It is constant and not afflicted or affected by the variableness of the earth. The constancy and veracity of the Word of God is emphasized here. Christian must find his comfort in the immutable and perfect Word of God. It is settled forever in heaven untouched by the whims and fancies of evil men. No matter how man may attack God's holy and perfect Word, it will never dent it or affect it. It is permanently secured by God Himself, settled forever in heaven. Be comforted and continue to trust the immutable God by trusting His inerrant, infallible and inspired and preserved perfect Word.

John Calvin observed correctly when he wrote, "Many explain this verse as if David adduced the stability of the heavens as a proof of God's truth. According to them the meaning is that God is proved to be true because the heavens continually remain in the same state. Others offer a still more forced interpretation, 'That God's truth is more sure than the state of the heavens.' But it appears to me that the prophet intended to convey a very different idea. **As we see nothing constant or of long continuance upon earth, he elevates our minds to heaven, that they may fix their anchor there**. David, no doubt, might have said, as he has done in many other places, that the whole order of the world bears testimony to the steadfastness of God's Word -- that Word which is most true. **But as there is reason to fear that the minds of the godly would hang in uncertainty if they rested the proof of God's truth upon the state of the world, in which such manifold disorders prevail; by placing God's truth in the heavens, he allots to it a habitation subject to no changes**. That no person then may estimate God's word from the various vicissitudes which meet his eye in this world, heaven is tacitly set in opposition to the earth. Our salvation, as if it had been said, being shut up in God's Word, is not subject to change, as all earthly things are, but is anchored in a safe and peaceful haven. The same truth the Prophet Isaiah teaches in somewhat different words: "All flesh is grass, and all the godliness thereof is as the flower of the field," (Isaiah 40:6).

"He means, according to the Apostle Peter's exposition, (1 Peter 1:24) that the certainty of salvation is to be sought in the Word, and, therefore that they do wrong who settle their minds upon the world; **for the steadfastness of God's Word far transcends the stability of the world**."

1 Peter 1:24-25, *"For all flesh is as grass, and all the glory of man as the flower of grass. The grass withereth, and the flower thereof falleth away: But the word of the Lord endureth for ever. And this is the word which by the gospel is preached unto you."*

The Psalmist did not stop at verse 89 but restates the same theme of verse 89 in the next two verses. Psalm 119:90-91 reads, *"Thy faithfulness is unto all generations: thou hast established the earth, and it abideth. They continue this day according to thine ordinances: for all are thy servants."* In the event that some might think that the Word of God is only constant in heaven and of no earthly good, verses 90 and 91 argue and answer this question. The earth may change but it changes within her own constancy. This constancy of the earth is in God's sovereign power and control. God revealed to us that this constancy of the earth's overall disposition has its foundation in the unchanging Word of God. It is according to the forever settled Word of God in heaven that the earth finds her constancy!

John Calvin is right when he commented that, ". . . the Psalmist repeats and confirms the same sentiment. He expressly teaches that although the faithful live for a short time as strangers upon earth, and soon pass away, yet their life is not perishable, since they are begotten again of an incorruptible seed. He, however, proceeds still farther. He had before enjoined us to peer by faith into heaven, because we will find nothing in the world on which we can assuredly rest; and now he again teaches us, by experience, that though the world is subject to revolutions, **yet in it bright and signal testimonies to the truth of God shine forth, so that the steadfastness of His Word is not exclusively confined to heaven, but comes down even to us who dwell upon the earth. For this reason, it is added, that the earth continues steadfast, even as it was established by God at the beginning**. Lord, as if it had been said, even in the earth we see Thy truth reflected as it were in a mirror; for though it is suspended in the midst of the sea, yet it continues to remain in the same state. **These two things, then, are quite consistent; first, that the steadfastness of God's Word is not to be judged of according to the condition of the world, which is always fluctuating, and fades away as a shadow; and, secondly, that yet men are ungrateful if they do not acknowledge the constancy which in many respects marks the framework of the world; for the earth, which otherwise could not occupy the position it does for a single moment, abides notwithstanding steadfast, because God's Word is the foundation on which it rests.** Farther, no person has any ground for objecting, that it is a hard thing to go beyond this world in quest of the evidences of God's truth, since, in that case, it would be too remote from the apprehension of men. The prophet meets the objection by affirming, **that although it dwells in heaven, yet we may see at our very feet conspicuous proofs of it, which may gradually advance us to as perfect knowledge of it as our limited capacity will permit. Thus the prophet, on the one hand, exhorts us to rise above the whole world by faith, so that the Word of God may be found by experience to be adequate, as it really is adequate, to sustain our faith; and, on the other hand, he warns us that we have no excuse, if, by the very sight of the earth, we do not discover the truth of God, since legible traces of it are to be found at our feet.** In the first clause, men are called back from the vanity of their own understanding; and, in the other; their weakness is relieved, that they

may have a foretaste upon earth of what is to be found more fully in heaven. [Taken from:
http://www.ccel.org/c/calvin/comment3/comm_vol11/htm/xxviii.xii.htm]

III. CONCLUSION

Let the comments of Spurgeon on Psalm 119:89 be our summary:
"The strain is more joyful, for experience has given the sweet singer a comfortable knowledge of the Word of the Lord, and this makes a glad theme. After tossing about on a sea of trouble, the Psalmist here leaps to shore and stands upon a rock. **Jehovah's Word is not fickle nor uncertain; it is settled, determined, fixed, sure, immovable. Man's teachings change so often that there is never time for them to be settled; but the Lord's Word is from of old the same, and will remain unchanged eternally.** Some men are never happier than when they are unsettling everything and everybody; but God's mind is not with them. **The power and glory of heaven have confirmed each sentence which the mouth of the Lord has spoken, and so confirmed it that to all eternity it must stand the same — settled in heaven, where nothing can reach it.** In the former section David's soul fainted, but here the good man looks out of self and perceives that the Lord fainteth not, neither is weary, neither is there any failure in His Word.

"The verse takes the form of an ascription of praise: the faithfulness and immutability of God are fit themes for holy song, and when we are tired with gazing upon the shifting scene of this life, the thought of the immutable promise fills our mouth with singing. **God's purposes, promises, and precepts are all settled in His own mind, and none of them shall be disturbed. Covenant settlements will not be removed, however unsettled the thoughts of men may become; let us therefore settle it in our minds that we abide in the faith of our Jehovah as long as we have any being.**"
[http://www.eternallifeministries.org/psalm119l.htm]

Two other verses that support the teaching of Psalm 119:89 are:

(a) Psalm 119:152: "*Concerning thy testimonies, I have known of old that thou hast founded them for ever.*"

(b) Psalm 119:160: "T*hy word is true from the beginning: and every one of thy righteous judgments endureth for ever.*"

LESSON 6

BIBLICAL SUPPORT IV

For The Doctrine of Verbal Plenary Preservation

Jesus Assures Preservation of the Bible

Matthew 5:17-19

I. INTRODUCTION

No Christian should hold on to any view that contradicts what Jesus has taught. Today, there is much confusion and contention among "Christian" teachers and leaders on the subject of the infallibility and preservation of the Scripture. But as committed Christians, we cannot afford to be confused or misled by false views concerning the Scripture, especially when Christ has unequivocally stated His view for us to hold on to. Jesus affirmed the infallibility and preservation of the Scripture by saying: "Think not that I am come to destroy the law, or the prophets: I am not come to destroy, but to fulfil. For verily I say unto you, Till heaven and earth pass, one jot or one tittle shall in no wise pass from the law, till all be fulfilled..." (Matthew 5:17-19). To understand Jesus' teaching on the infallibility and preservation of the Scripture, we shall study His words found in Matthew 5:17-19.

Matthew records these words of Christ as part of the Sermon on the Mount. In verse 18, for the first time in His sermon, Jesus used the authoritative and dogmatic formula "I say unto you;" and He repeats it again in verse 20: "For I say unto you ..." This suggests to us that Jesus really expects our total attention on the words that follow so that we may study them and observe them as cardinal doctrine and practice. There should be no contention about these explicit words of Jesus about the Scripture. His view about the Scripture, expressed in Matthew 5:17-19, should be our view always.

It would be very helpful if we can recollect the historical and scriptural background of the passage under our consideration to get the real feel of its emphasis.

II. HISTORICAL AND SCRIPTURAL BACKGROUND

A. Historical Background

Since John the Baptist introduced Christ to the world, the eyes of everyone in Israel were upon Him. He appeared to be very different from the scribes and Pharisees. He did not follow the prevailing theology of His day and refused to identify Himself with any of the sects of His time. He disregarded their traditions as well as their extraneous and legalistic rules. As a friend of publicans and sinners, He proclaimed love and grace. His meekness and humility made Him distinguishable from all other religious teachers who were proud, boastful and hypocritical. He preached forgiveness of sins and dispensed mercy. Consequently, the people and the Jewish leaders wondered if He was destroying all the absolutes of the Old Testament Scripture for some new teaching. Many were inclined to think that He intended to subvert the the authority of God's Word.

So Jesus came forward to remove their doubts and said, in effect, "What you see and hear is nothing new at all. I did not come to remove the Old Testament law but to reiterate and fulfil it." So His amazing manifesto is in direct harmony with the Old Testament, though it was in direct confrontation with their thinking. When the scribes and Pharisees were making the traditions binding upon people, Jesus was talking about grace and mercy. But Jesus told them that they had dragged the divine standard so low that it was necessary to raise it again. Having a greater commitment to the law than the most scrupulous scribe or Pharisee, Jesus proceeded to support the unfailing and lasting authority of the Scripture.

B. Scriptural Context

In Matthew 5:3-12, Jesus gives a list of the characteristics of a true Christian. Then, in verses 13 and 16, He emphasized what a true believer ought to be and how he should act. From verses 17 to 20, Jesus shows how it is possible to be like what He taught us to be. Here He shows us how to live out the Beatitudes and be the salt and light in a decaying and darkened world; certainly not by lowering God's standard that is written, but by striving to live in complete obedience to all that God has revealed, even to the jot and tittle. This was, obviously, a shocking appeal to the society of Jesus' day, which obeyed only what it wanted to

Jesus introduces the key to a righteous life as nothing else but keeping of God's law. The only way to have true righteousness is to go beyond the phony externalism of the scribes and Pharisees, to the inward righteousness that is only wrought by the power and authority of God's Word. Therefore, when Jesus came, He did not abolish the Old Testament but He reinforced it.

III. JESUS ADHERES HIMSELF TO THE WHOLE OF SCRIPTURE

To understand how extensive and emphatic Jesus' declaration of His view of the Scripture is, the words He used must be carefully considered. First of all, what did Jesus mean when He referred to the law or the prophets? The term "law" can be a reference to the Ten Commandments or the first five books of Moses, or to the whole Old Testament. But usually, the Jews used the word when they were talking about the oral scribal traditions that they had been receiving from various rabbis.

Now when Jesus said, "Think not that I am come to destroy the law...," He was not talking about the traditions of men. By using the definite article "the law," the multitude should have understood that Jesus was talking about the law of God. But how do we know whether Jesus was referring to the Ten Commandments or the Pentateuch or the whole Old Testament? Verse 17 settles it, when it says: "the law, or the prophets." In the Gospel of Matthew, "the law and the prophets" is used four times (Matthew 5:17; 7:12; 11:13; 22:40), with reference to the whole of the Old Testament. Therefore, we can confidently say that "the law" in this passage in Matthew 5 refers to the whole Old Testament.

Interestingly, in 5:17 "the law" and "prophets" are not connected by the conjunction "and" (Greek *kai*) as in the other three places mentioned above. Here instead of *kai*, Matthew uses the adversative "or" (Greek *e*). Lenski comments: The "adversative" divides the Old Testament into two parts: "The law" or Pentateuch; "the prophets" or all the rest of the

Old Testament. In other words, the word "or" implies that the attitude taken by Christ is the same towards both. Thus, Jesus most emphatically proclaims His full adherence to the whole of the Old Testament.

Another term that stresses His total adherence to the Scripture is "fulfil," when He said: "I am not come to destroy, but to fulfil" (5:17). Now the question before us is – In what way did Christ fulfil "the law" and "the prophets?" Many commentators argue that Christ fulfilled the law and the prophets in two different ways. The prophets are fulfilled in a predictive fashion: what they predict comes to pass and is thereby fulfilled. The law, some say, is fulfilled by confirming the law in its deeper meaning while others say Jesus fulfilled the law by dying on the cross, thus satisfying the demands of the law against all who would believe in Him. Though these ideas are established elsewhere in the New Testament, the emphasis that Matthew conveys is more extensive. Elsewhere, Matthew records Jesus as saying, "For all the prophets and the law prophesied until John" (Matthew 11:13). Not only do the prophets prophesy, but the law also prophesies. In other words, the entire Old Testament has a prophetic function and Jesus came to fulfil the Old Testament. In Matthew 5:17, therefore, we must rid ourselves of conceptions of fulfilment which are too narrow. Jesus fulfilled the entire Old Testament – the law and the prophets, in many ways. Because they point towards Him, He had certainly not come to abolish them, but rather, to fulfil them in a rich diversity of ways. In summary, we can say that Jesus' life and ministry were not in opposition to the Old Testament, but in fulfillment of all that it says.

IV. JESUS AFFIRMS THAT EVERY LETTER OF THE SCRIPTURE WILL BE PRESERVED

Thus, after declaring His total adherence to the Scripture, He states His view of the Scripture: "For verily I say unto you, Till heaven and earth pass, one jot or one tittle shall in no wise pass from the law, till all be fulfilled" (verse 18). As we noticed before, "the law" in this verse also refers to the entire Old Testament. It would be unwarranted if we say "the law" refers only to the legal requirements, especially when we study verse 18 in the light of verse 17. Thus, referring to the entire Old Testament, He wishes to make a strong assertion when He says, "For verily I say unto you." The word "verily" is a translation of the Greek term "amen" which is a transliteration of the Hebrew word for "truth." Therefore, it generally identifies something true, faithful or absolute.

This expression, thus, explains to us how highly Jesus regards the Scripture, and how important the following statement is of His view of the Scripture - "Till heaven and earth pass, one jot or one tittle shall in no wise pass from the law, till all be fulfilled."

Jesus then tells us how long the Scripture will continue to be unerring and authoritative - "till heaven and earth pass." In other words, Jesus was emphasizing the relative imperishability of God's Word, by saying that it would be here even when the universe passed out of its present existence.

Then He continues to express His view in the most exhaustive way by saying, "one jot or one tittle shall in no wise pass from the law, till all be fulfilled." A "jot" (or *yodh*) refers to the smallest letter of the Hebrew alphabet, which is very similar to an apostrophe. A "tittle" is an appendage or portion of the letter, a mark by which one letter is distinguished from another. So what Jesus is saying is that not even the tiniest Hebrew letter shall pass from this law until all would be fulfilled.

If God does not preserve every letter of the Scripture, then the truth of God's Word would be lost. The purity and authority of the whole Scripture are dependent on every section of the Scripture, every book, every chapter, every word, and every letter. Even the smallest letter or a portion of a letter cannot be lost, if the authority and infallibility of the Scripture have to remain unaffected all through time. The Lord Jesus assures us that His Word will be preserved true to every letter. We may have difficulty in understanding how the Lord could speak of absolutely perfect preservation of the Scripture in its originals, when there were cases of scribal errors in manuscripts. Though scribal errors have occurred in some copies, the Lord promises to keep His Word free from all such human errors for His people to believe and obey.

Today, we have no need to approach the Scripture with doubt. It is divinely preserved from all impurity. Through the history of the church, we can see how God providentially guided godly men not only to determine the books of the canon of the Scripture, but also to recognize the exact original words of those books for an obedient life. In the Hebrew and Greek texts underlying the King James Bible, we have these perfectly preserved texts through the ages, recognized by godly men during the days of the Reformation, and continued to be used by the church for the past 400 years approximately. A perfectly preserved Bible to the end of times – that is what the Lord Jesus promised in Matthew 5:18, and that is what we have today.

V. JESUS WARNS US NOT TO DISREGARD EVEN THE LEAST COMMANDMENT OF THE SCRIPTURE

Because every letter of the Scripture will be preserved to the end of days, Jesus warns us about setting aside or disannulling any portion of the Scripture. "Whosoever therefore shall break one of these least commandments, and shall teach men so, he shall be called the least in the kingdom of heaven: but whosoever shall do and teach them, the same shall be called great in the kingdom of heaven" (verse 19). The word "therefore" takes our attention backward, and gives us one reason why we should not disregard the Scripture. The reason is, as we found earlier, that God's Word is imperishable.

Then Jesus forewarns us of the consequences, if we disregard even a smallest portion of His Word – "Whosoever therefore shall break one of these least commandments, and shall teach men so, he shall be called the least in the kingdom of heaven." The word "break" (Greek *luo*) means "to loose, release, nullify or destroy." Therefore, the idea conveyed is if anyone releases himself from an obligation to obey or to teach exactly what it says, even the least of it, he will be called the least in the kingdom of heaven. This suggests that such men will face the Lord's judgment for unbelief and loss of reward.

Another significant phrase that should be noticed is "these commandments." The expression "these commandments" must be understood within the context since any expressed antecedent for the term "these" is absent. In the previous verses, Jesus referred to the whole Old Testament and claimed that He came not to destroy but to fulfil them. Since Jesus is the fulfillment of "the law" and "the prophets" (or the whole Old Testament points to Him), our responsibility is not only to obey the commandments of the Old Testament but also His teachings as found in the New Testament. We must also take heed of the words of the New Testament writers for they were written as inspired by His Spirit.

VI. CONCLUSION

In this passage, we have seen how our Lord promises to preserve all the letters of His Word that His people may have an infallible, everlasting Scripture. As disciples of Jesus, we must also hold the same view of the Scripture, which Jesus proclaimed. To doubt the perfect preservation of the Bible, as many have done, is to simply deny Jesus' promise. That would also mean to drift away from the perfect standard of righteousness. The message the Lord gives in Matthew 5:17-19 is: Fulfil God's law, and do not break even the least of His commandments, because His Word is pre-eminent, permanent and pertinent till the end of days. All Christians must affirm their allegiance to the Word of God. If anyone, therefore, questions its perfect preservation, infallibility and authority, he cannot be considered a faithful Christian, let alone a faithful Bible teacher. Dear reader, it is time for us to take heed of our Saviour's words more than ever before, and uphold His perfect Word by believing, obeying and proclaiming all of its words.

VII. IF WE REJECT THE DOCTRINE OF THE PRESERVATION OF THE BIBLE

Rejecting the Doctrine of the Perfect Preservation of the Bible will lead to many severe spiritual dangers. It will undermine the very foundation of the Christian faith. The following are the dangerous outcomes of not believing in the Perfect Preservation of the Bible.

If we reject the Perfect Preservation of the Bible, then we concede that:

1. We don't have the inspired Word of God intact, as the words of the originals are not kept pure (cf. 2 Timothy 3:16).

2. We don't have an absolutely infallible, inerrant Word of God, even though the Lord promises a perfect Word of God forever (cf. Psalm 19:7-9).

3. God is unfaithful in keeping His repeated promise that He will preserve His Word forever (cf. Psalm 12:6-7; Psalm 111:7-8; Psalm 119:89, 152, 160).

4. Jesus' promises, such as, "my words shall not pass away," are unreliable (Matthew 24:35; Mark 13:31; Luke 21:33).

5. Jesus did not mean what He said, because the Bible is not preserved as He uttered - "Till heaven and earth pass, one jot or one tittle shall in no wise pass from the law, till all be fulfilled" (Matthew 5:18; cf. Luke 16:17)

6. God was so incapacitated by the errors of man and dark events of history that He failed to keep His promises concerning the Preservation of His Word. (It also casts doubt on God's sovereignty, providence, omnipotence, omniscience, etc.)

7. The faith of the Old Testament prophets and saints that God's Word will be kept intact forever is a false faith. "The grass withereth, the flower fadeth: but the word of our God shall stand for ever" (Isaiah 40:8). "The fear of the LORD is clean, enduring for ever: the judgments of the LORD are true and righteous altogether" (Psalm 19:9).

8. The affirmation of the apostles of Christ and the New Testament writers that God's Word will be kept intact forever is false. (Matthew, Mark and Luke quoted Jesus' affirmation of the Preservation of God's Word, cf. 1 Peter 1:25).

9. Our forefathers' faith that the Word of God "by His singular care and providence, kept pure in all ages" is not acceptable (Westminster Confession of Faith I.VIII).

10. Anyone can question the authenticity and authority of the words in the Bible (cf. John 17:17).

11. Some parts of the Bible must be subjected to the "scholarly opinion" of certain individuals. When those intellectuals point to us where the Bible is allegedly wrong, we should believe them more than the Bible itself (cf. Matthew 5:17-19).

12. It is wrong to have the presupposition that believers have an absolutely trustworthy, perfect Bible (cf. Psalm 18:30; Psalm 111:7-8; Psalm 119:128).

Denying the Perfect Preservation of the Bible will harm and hurt the Church. It will open the door for anyone to criticize the text of the Bible according to his personal thinking or opinion. This will further lead to doubting the absolute accuracy and authority of the Bible. Thus the very foundation of the church, the absolute sufficiency, trustworthiness and authority of the Bible will be weakened and destroyed. If we preachers do not have a perfectly preserved Bible, what assurance can the hearers have in our preaching of the Word? If we do not have a perfectly preserved Bible, our preaching is vain.

LESSON 7

The King James Bible And The Doctrine of Verbal Plenary Preservation

I. INTRODUCTION

What is the relationship between the King James Bible and the doctrine of Verbal Plenary Preservation of God's Word? The answer is simple. The King James Bible accurately preserves God's divine words in the Hebrew and Greek languages by accurately translating these words into the English language.

To avoid confusion and misunderstanding of the matter, it is necessary to clarify that VPP proponents believe God has preserved for His people His 100% Perfect Hebrew and Greek words. And these are the Hebrew and Greek words that underlie the King James Bible. The King James Bible is only a translation. No translated words can be better than the inspired Hebrew and Greek words given by God.

When using the KJB, it is necessary to go back to the words in the original languages for clarity and fullness of meaning. By way of illustration, the words in the original languages underlying the KJB are like the perfect platinum ruler of the Smithsonian Institute, inerrant, infallible, and authoritative. The KJB and other accurate and reliable translations are like the common ruler, though not perfect, are good and safe enough for use.

In this study, we shall look at how we got our King James Bible and how the King James Bible is superior in four areas (Texts, Translators, Techniques, Theology) as compared to all the other modern English Bible translations today.

II. THE BOOK OF BOOKS ... HOW WE GOT THE KING JAMES BIBLE [1]

No book is like the Bible: it is the BOOK of books. Its words are "God-breathed," inspired. *"All scripture is given by inspiration of God . . ."* (2 Tim 3:16). God was the unseen Author; the men who wrote were amanuenses. 2 Peter 1:19–21 says,

> *For we have also a more sure word of prophecy; . . .. Knowing this first, that no prophecy of the scripture is of any private interpretation. For the prophecy came not in old time by the will of man: but holy men of God spake as they were moved by the Holy Ghost.*

In old time God spoke, and holy men wrote. To John the Apostle it was given to *"bare record of the word of God, and of the testimony of Jesus Christ . . ."* (Rev 1:2). Our Lord, the One that sat upon the Throne, said to John: *"Write: for these words are true and faithful"* (Rev 21:5). The **spoken words** are preserved for us through the ages, as the **written words** in the Bible, a sure record that withstands the ravages of time and decay

The original records of God's words, the AUTOGRAPHS, were written in Hebrew (almost all of the Old Testament) and Greek (New Testament). Today the *autographs* are long gone through years of hard usage. But copies of God's words are still with us. Thanks be unto God for preserving His words in the thousands of Hebrew and Greek manuscripts by the hands of faithful men. God has not left Himself without a witness.

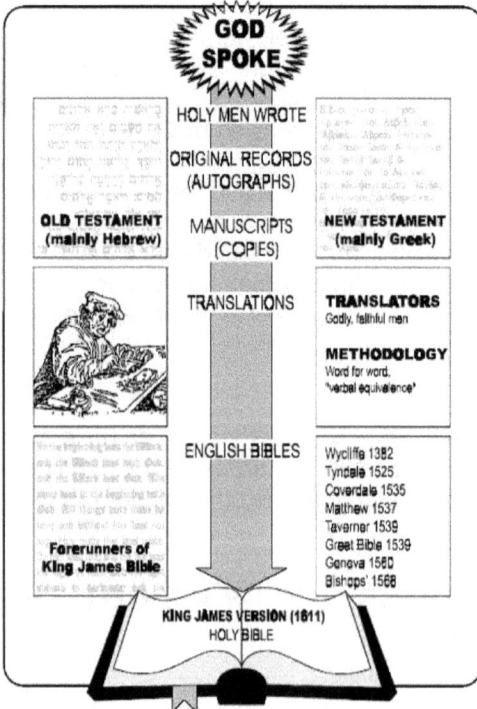

HOW WE GOT OUR BIBLE (KJV)

GOD SPOKE

HOLY MEN WROTE

ORIGINAL RECORDS (AUTOGRAPHS)

OLD TESTAMENT (mainly Hebrew)

MANUSCRIPTS (COPIES)

NEW TESTAMENT (mainly Greek)

TRANSLATIONS

TRANSLATORS
Godly, faithful men

METHODOLOGY
Word for word,
"verbal equivalence"

ENGLISH BIBLES

Wycliffe 1382
Tyndale 1525
Coverdale 1535
Matthew 1537
Taverner 1539
Great Bible 1539
Geneva 1560
Bishops' 1568

Forerunners of King James Bible

KING JAMES VERSION (1611)
HOLY BIBLE

The Word of God is not to be bound, but must be published to all people, that they may obtain salvation by Jesus Christ. For this purpose God raised up godly men of wisdom and learning, to translate His Word into many languages. Our discussion here focuses on the English translations, not the non-English translations.

John Wycliffe was the first to give the English people a translation in their own tongue (1382), but it was based on the *Latin Vulgate* (a Latin Bible translated from Hebrew and Greek). **William Tyndale** was the first to produce an English translation from the original Greek and Hebrew texts (1525), for which he suffered martyrdom. Other translations followed, based on the same Hebrew and Greek texts: *Coverdale* (1535), *Matthew* (1537), *Taverner* (1539), *the Great Bible* (1539), *the Geneva* (1560), *the Bishops'* (1568).

These translations were useful as forerunners of the *King James Version* (KJB) or *Authorized Version* (AV) of 1611. Within a short time of its appearance, the KJB was acknowledged as the superior and unrivalled translation. This was due to the superior scholarship of the translators: a team of the best scholars from Oxford and Cambridge, who were godly men with a high view of the Scriptures, fully committed to the accurate and faithful rendering of God's eternal Word from the original languages into the best classical English. The KJB or Authorized Version (AV) is the Twenty-First Century English Reader's Bible. We present this Book to our readers as THE one English translation which, above all other English Bibles, is the most complete, accurate and faithful English translation of the original inspired words of God. With the KJB, the reader will not be deceived in any matters that God has chosen to reveal to us through His inspired words.

III. A FOUR-FOLD SUPERIORITY OF THE KING JAMES BIBLE [2]

A. Superior Original Language Texts

The textual foundation of the King James Bible is the best compared to that used by all other English Bibles that exist today. The King James Old Testament is translated from the Traditional Masoretic Hebrew Old Testament text (Ben Chayyim). The Masoretes handed down this text from generation to generation, guarded it and kept it well. The majority of the modern English versions, however, were translated from other Hebrew texts like Rudolph Kittel's Biblia Hebraica, Samaritan

Pentateuch, etc., which are different from the Traditional Masoretic Text. If the Hebrew foundation of the modern English versions and the King James Bible are different, how can their translated English words be the same? Surely, they cannot be the same. They are different. Why is the Old Testament Hebrew Text of the King James Bible superior? It is superior because: Firstly, it was preserved by the Jews. Secondly, the traditional text of the Jews was Authorized by Jesus. He has never refuted any text, any word or any letter in the Hebrew Old Testament

He stamped His authorization on the Masoretic Hebrew Text. He did not give His approval on the Septuagint, the Latin Vulgate, some scribal tradition, Josephus, Jerome, the Syriac version or any other document present at that time! In Matthew 5:18, Jesus said, "*Till heaven and earth pass, one jot or one tittle shall in no wise pass from the law, till all be fulfilled.*" This proves that our Lord believes in the preservation of the Scripture to the extent that every word of it has been kept intact.

The King James Bible is also based on a superior Greek New Testament, the Textus Receptus. The chief opponent of the Textus Receptus is the Nestle/Aland Greek New Testament 26th edition, which is used in most colleges, universities, and seminaries today (even conservative and/or fundamental ones). The editors of this corrupt Greek Text were made up of a committee comprising unbelievers, a Roman Catholic Cardinal, and apostates. Basically, it is this same Greek Text that underlies almost all modern English versions.

The Textus Receptus that underlies the King James Bible, however, was received by the Church for almost 1,800 years until 1881 when Westcott and Hort's Greek Text came into the scene. Since then, almost all preachers studied this corrupt Greek Text, but still preached out of the King James Bible (which was based on a different Greek text). Later, even the King James Bible was kicked out in favour of English Bibles that are based on the "preferred" corrupt Greek text.

B. Superior Translators

The King James translators were men of great spiritual insight. They believed that people need to read the Bible, and therefore, there was a need for proper translation of the Scripture.

There were fifty-seven translators, divided into six teams. They met in three cities, namely, Cambridge, Westminster and Oxford. They began their work in 1604 and completed it in 1611. In both Westminster and Oxford, the translators focused on the Old Testament and New Testament. In Cambridge, they had a team working with the Old Testament and Apocrypha. Even though the translators included the Apocrypha in the original King James Bible, they did not believe it was inspired. Therefore, they translated it as history between the Old and New Testaments. Dr. John Reynolds, a devout puritan, led this great work of translation from the beginning to the end.

Many of them possessed superb language skills and were known for their expertise in Hebrew, Greek and English. They applied their skills and did excellently in the translation. With all these fifty-seven superior translators, we can be assured of the superiority of their product.

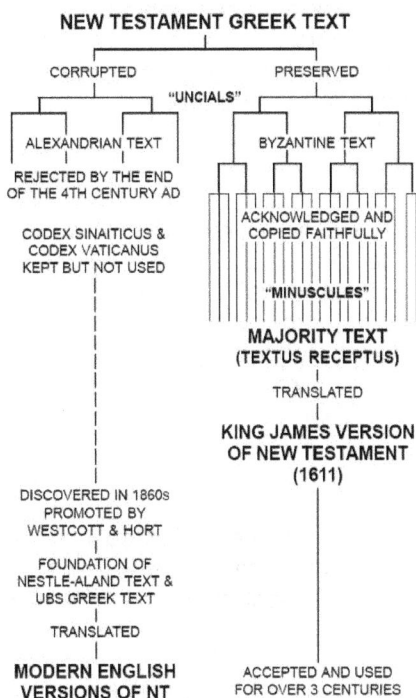

NEW TESTAMENT GREEK TEXT

CORRUPTED

PRESERVED

"UNCIALS"

ALEXANDRIAN TEXT

BYZANTINE TEXT

REJECTED BY THE END
OF THE 4TH CENTURY AD

ACKNOWLEDGED AND
COPIED FAITHFULLY

CODEX SINAITICUS &
CODEX VATICANUS
KEPT BUT NOT USED

"MINUSCULES"

MAJORITY TEXT
(TEXTUS RECEPTUS)

TRANSLATED

KING JAMES VERSION
OF NEW TESTAMENT
(1611)

DISCOVERED IN 1860s
PROMOTED BY
WESTCOTT & HORT

FOUNDATION OF
NESTLE-ALAND TEXT &
UBS GREEK TEXT

TRANSLATED

MODERN ENGLISH
VERSIONS OF NT

ACCEPTED AND USED
FOR OVER 3 CENTURIES

C. Superior Technique

There are two aspects to the superior technique used by the translators of the King James Bible: Superior Team Technique, and Superior Translation Technique.

The King James Bible was translated differently from other modern English versions. Each translator had to translate the books on his own, unaided by anyone else. Every translator on the six teams, fifty-seven of them, had to be so skilled in the Hebrew or Greek books assigned him that he had to translate all of them by himself in his own handwriting. In addition, they had a total of fifteen rules to govern their translation work.

They had a **team technique** that is unequalled by any modern translators. This is how they do it. They had about seven translators in a team. One translator is assigned to one book. For each completed book, it had to be examined by the other six translators individually, and one more time meeting together to go over it to decide which translated words would stand – in total eight times. Then it will be sent to the other five teams for vetting – that is five more times and at the end they had a joint meeting of two men from each of the six teams – twelve men. That makes a total of fourteen different times for one book. That was how they translated, analysed and corrected in their translation from Genesis to Revelation. This technique was a team effort and certainly superior without any doubt!

The **translation technique** adopted by the King James translators is the verbal and formal translation technique. This method is the translation of Hebrew and Greek words as closely as possible into English. Every noun, adjective, preposition, participle and so on in the Hebrew and Greek text is brought into the English in the same way. That includes the structure and form as well. Dynamic equivalence is directly opposite of the verbal and formal equivalence technique. It is not a word-for-word translation. The words were either added, changed or subtracted in the English. This is also known as "paraphrasing."

Should not God's Word be read in English exactly as we would find in the Hebrew and Greek texts? We can see this in the King James Bible which has been translated by the verbal and formal equivalence technique, but not in other modern versions which used the dynamic equivalence technique that mixes God's words with man's words. Indeed we can confidently trust that the King James Bible is God's Word accurately translated into English.

D. Superior Theology

There are those who say that no vital doctrine is affected in the modern English versions. This claim is clearly false. There are two possible ways theology (or doctrines) can be affected in the modern English versions:

(1) through the translators' paraphrasing in the modern English version

(2) through the corrupt Greek text used.

Theology is affected in the modern English versions when important words in the Greek text are changed or omitted. The followings are just some examples how theology has been affected:

a. The Doctrine of Holy Trinity

1 John 5:7 (KJB based on the TR): "For there are three that bear record *in heaven, the Father, the Word, and the Holy Ghost: and these three are one.*"

1 John 5:8 (KJB based on TR): "*And there are three that bear witness in earth*, the spirit, and the water, and the blood: and these three agree in one."

1 John 5:7 and 8 are one of the clearest biblical support for the Doctrine of the Holy Trinity.

Yet, the italicized portions are **eliminated** from the corrupt Greek texts (Codex Vaticanus and Codex Sinaiticus) and are therefore not found in the modern English versions that are based on these corrupt Greek texts. Egs of such English versions are the NIV, NASV, and NKJB. This is certainly a matter of doctrine and theology. The corrupt Greek texts and their subsequent English translations are theologically deficient, whereas the Textus Receptus and, subsequently, the King James Bible are theologically superior.

b. The Doctrine of the Judgment

2 Peter 3:10 (KJB based on the TR): "But the day of the Lord will come as a thief in the night; in the which the heavens shall pass away with a great noise, and the elements shall melt with fervent heat, the earth also and the works that are therein shall be *burned up.*"

The italicized portion is **altered** in the corrupt Greek texts (Codex Vaticanus and Codex Sinaiticus) and their subsequent English translations (NIV, NKJB). Instead of the words "burned up," the words "laid bare" are used. There is a vast difference between "burned up" and "laid bare." The word "laid bare" is an entirely different concept and word picture. This is no clear description of how hell is to be like.

This is certainly a matter of doctrine and theology. There corrupt Greek texts and their subsequent English translations are theologically deficient, whereas the Textus Receptus and, subsequently, the King James Bible are theologically superior.

c. The Doctrine of the Christ

Luke 2:22 (KJB based on the TR): "And when the days of *her* purification according to the law of Moses were accomplished, they brought him to Jerusalem, to present him to the Lord."

The italicized portion is **changed** in the Greek texts (Codex Vaticanus and Codex Sinaiticus) and their subsequent English translations (NIV, NASV, NB). The word "her" is changed to "their," thus making the Lord Jesus Christ One who needed "purification," and therefore a sinner! This is unthinkable!

This is certainly a matter of doctrine and theology. These Greek texts and their subsequent English translations are theologically deficient, whereas the Textus Receptus and, subsequently, the King James Bible are theologically superior.

Other theological doctrines affected that are either **eliminated, altered** or **changed** are the doctrine of the church (Revelation 2:15), the doctrine of angels (Luke 22:43), the doctrine of Satan (Luke 4:8), the doctrine of the Bible (Mark 16:9-20; John 7:53-8:11; etc.), the doctrine of last things or prophecy (Matthew 25:13; Mark 12:23; etc.), the doctrine of salvation (Revelation 21:24; 1 Peter 2:2; etc.), and the doctrine of Christ (John 3:13; 1 Corinthians 11:24; etc.).

Theology is indeed affected and undermined in the modern English versions today. How can the whole counsel of God be faithfully taught in these modern English perversions?

IV. THE GREEK SOURCE TEXT OF MODERN ENGLISH BIBLES [3]

The subject has been well researched and documented by the Trinitarian Bible Society of England in *"The Divine Original."* We can do no better than quote from it:

The Vatican and Sinai Manuscripts

In the mid-nineteenth century the Codex Sinaiticus and Codex Vaticanus became available to Biblical scholars, and in 1881 Westcott and Hort advanced the theory that the New Testament text was preserved in an almost perfect state in these two fourth century manuscripts.

The discovery of these MSS betrayed many Biblical students into a lamentable infirmity of critical judgment. Tischendorf himself, the discoverer of the Sinai Codex, amended his eighth edition in at least 3,505 places in conformity with new readings which he found in this document. The Codex Vaticanus exercised a similar mesmeric influence on the minds of many 19th and 20th century scholars. The Revised Greek Text underlying the modern versions has the support only of that very small minority of the available MSS which are in some respects in agreement with the unreliable text of the Sinai and Vatican codices.

An Elaborate Theory

Westcott and Hort devised an elaborate theory, based more on imagination and intuition than upon evidence, elevating this little group of MSS to the heights of almost infallible authority. Their treatise on the subject and their edition of the Greek NT exercised a powerful and far-reaching influence, not only on the next generation of students and scholars, but also indirectly upon the minds of millions who have had neither the ability, nor the time, nor the inclination to submit the theory to a searching examination.

Doctrinal Deficiencies of these MSS

These two MSS and a few others containing a similar text present in a weakened form many passages of Holy Scripture which speak most plainly of the deity of the Son of God. The trend of Biblical scholarship in the 19th and 20th centuries has been towards a "humanitarian" view of the person of Christ. It is not surprising that many modern scholars should welcome the support of these two ancient documents, but it is sad to see so many earnest evangelical Christians ready to accept without question a theory so destructive of the faith once delivered to the saints.

The True Text

The Sinai and Vatican manuscripts represent a small family of documents containing various readings which the Church as a whole rejected before the end of the 4th century. Under the singular care and providence of God more reliable MSS were multiplied and copied from generation to generation, and the great majority of existing MSS exhibit a faithful reproduction of the true text which was acknowledged by the entire Greek Church in the Byzantine period A.D. 312–1453. . . . This text is represented by the Authorized Version and other Protestant translations up to the latter part of the 19th century. [4]

The foregoing revelation by the Trinitarian Bible Society is simply devastating!

In the critical assessment of ancient Bible texts, we must rely on trustworthy experts in the fields. No one was better qualified than the brilliant linguist and Bible scholar John William Burgon (1813–1888). A man of rare integrity and fidelity to Holy Scripture, he was alarmed by the rising wave of antagonism against the Word of God.

Burgon, determined to unravel the truth about the newly discovered texts, went to Rome in 1860 to examine the *Codex Vaticanus* and to Mount Sinai to acquaint himself with St. Catherine's monastery where the *Codex Sinaiticus* was found.

A meticulous student, Burgon gave himself wholly to extensive study of Greek manuscripts, to research in the textual field, in order to be adequately equipped to defend the Bible under attack.

We quote from David Cloud's publication, *Modern Bible Versions*:

"Of the Sinaiticus and Vaticanus and the textual theories which exalt these manuscripts, the brilliant John Burgon, after decades of lonely, vigilant toil in the dim corners of Britain, Europe, and Egypt, testified:

"On first seriously applying ourselves to these studies, many years ago...turn which way we would, we were encountered by the same confident terminology: 'the best documents,' 'primary manuscripts,' 'first-rate authorities,' 'primitive evidence,' 'ancient readings,' and so forth: *we found that thereby codices* א *[Sinaiticus] or B [Vaticanus], codices C or D [two similar manuscripts] were invariably and exclusively meant.* It was not until we had laboriously collated these documents for ourselves, that we became aware of their true character. Long before coming to the end of our task (and it occupied us, off and on, for eight years) we had become convinced that the supposed 'best documents' and 'first-rate authorities' are in reality among the worst.

"A diligent inspection of a vast number of later copies scattered throughout the principal libraries of Europe, and the exact collation of a few, further convinced us that the deference generally claimed for B, ℵ, C, D is nothing else but a weak superstition and a vulgar error, that the date for a MS is not of its essence, but is a mere accident of the problem, and that *later copies…on countless occasions, and as a rule, preserve those delicate lineaments and minute refinements which the 'old uncials' are constantly observed to obliterate.* And so, rising to a systematic survey of the entire field of Evidence, we found reason to suspect more and more the soundness of the conclusions at which Lachmann, Tregelles, and Tischendorf had arrived: while we seemed led, as if by the hand, to discern plain indications of the existence for ourselves of a far 'more excellent way' (*Revision Revised*, pp. 337, 338).

"We suspect that these two manuscripts [Sinaiticus and Vaticanus] are indebted for their preservation, solely to their ascertained evil character; which has occasioned that the one eventually found its way, four centuries ago, to a forgotten shelf in the Vatican library; while the other, after exercising the ingenuity of several generations of critical correctors, eventually got deposited in the waste-paper basket of the convent at the foot of Mount Sinai. Had these been copies of average purity, they must long since have shared the inevitable fate of books which are freely used and highly prized; namely, they would have fallen into decadence and disappeared from sight (*Revision Revised*, p. 319)."

Thus we see that during the 1800s, one of the greatest missionary eras in history, while godly men were carrying the preserved Bible to the ends of the earth, unbelieving textual critics, enamoured by German rationalism, went about searching the dusty libraries of apostate institutions to rediscover the Word of God that had never been lost! [5]

These two MSS fell into the hands of Westcott and Hort, two unregenerate professors in Cambridge, who promptly elevated them to a place of authority, lending the weight of their names to the texts.

V. TWO ANGLICAN CHURCHMEN FROM CAMBRIDGE [6]

Soon after the discovery of the *Codex Sinaiticus* and *Codex Vaticanus*, two learned professors, Westcott and Hort, Anglican Churchmen from Cambridge, got to work on these defective manuscripts. Out of them they published their edition of the Greek NT which was then presented to the world as the **most accurate, authentic** and **trustworthy**.

With their stamp of authority, their Greek NT literally captured the imagination of the scholastic community. Since then the *Westcott-Hort Greek NT* has dominated the field of NT Greek scholars and translators around the world. By one fell stroke the TR (*Textus Receptus* or Majority Text) was dethroned, and the *Westcott-Hort* (W-H) text was seated in the chair of authority. While these two men and their followers exalt their text as "the best," another school (as we have seen) rejects them as "the worst." What does God's Word say on the matter? Our Lord's teaching from the "Sermon on the Mount" (Matt 7:15–18) applies:

Beware of false prophets, which come to you in sheep's clothing, but inwardly they are ravening wolves. Ye shall know them by their fruits. Do men gather grapes of thorns, or figs of thistles? Even so every good tree bringeth forth good fruit; but a corrupt tree bringeth forth evil fruit. A good tree cannot bring forth evil fruit, neither can a corrupt tree bring forth good fruit.

Then says the Apostle James: "Doth a fountain send forth at the same place sweet water and bitter? Can the fig tree . . . bear olive berries? . . . so can no fountain both yield salt water and fresh" (Jas 3:11–12).

What sort of "tree" and "fountain" are Westcott and Hort? What are their doctrinal beliefs and persuasion? These have been subjected to a penetrating analysis in Heresies of Westcott and Hort by D A Waite. Behind their academic gowns and "evangelical" façade, the real Westcott and Hort harboured a secret affection for Rome and the Virgin Mary. By their own writings the men reveal their true selves: unregenerate, strangers to the saving grace of God, and enemies of the Gospel of Jesus Christ. Hereat we present incontrovertible proof of the unbelief and anti-Christian position of Westcott and Hort, summarised from Waite's book.[7]

Denials of Basic Bible Truth by Westcott and Hort

Whether jointly or individually, Westcott and Hort, by their own pens, have denied or attacked the following fundamental doctrines of "*the faith which was once delivered unto the saints*" (Jude 3).

Westcott and Hort DENIED:

a   the doctrine of the inspiration of Scripture,

b   the Genesis record of the Creation and the Fall of man,

c   the Deity of our Lord Jesus Christ, His eternal pre-existence and Godhead, His Messiahship, and His sinlessness,

d   the substitutionary atonement of Christ and redemption by His blood,

e   the bodily resurrection of our Lord Jesus Christ,

f   the Second Coming of Christ,

g   the doctrine of Eternal Life,

h   the reality of Heaven and Hell,

i   the personality of the Devil.

Westcott and Hort BELIEVED IN:

a   the inherent goodness and perfectibility of man,

b   the Darwinian theory of Evolution,

c   the Universal Fatherhood of God,

d   the ultimate salvation of all men,

e   the efficacy of water baptism for Regeneration.

Westcott and Hort were **false prophets, ravening wolves in sheep's clothing** (Matt 7:15) "*deceitful workers*, transforming themselves into ... ministers of righteousness" (2 Cor 11:13-15). Their theories of Textual Criticism are false and must be utterly rejected. Their NT Greek Text is therefore also to be utterly rejected as pernicious poison. And yet a hundred new Bibles have flowed from this corrupt source.

GOOD FRUIT

One Version
KJV
Holy Bible

VITAL DOCTRINES PRESERVED

Deity of Christ

Virgin Birth of Christ

Redemption by the
Blood of the Lamb

GOOD TREE

Godly Translators

Good Technique

Textus Receptus

Good Text
Majority MSS

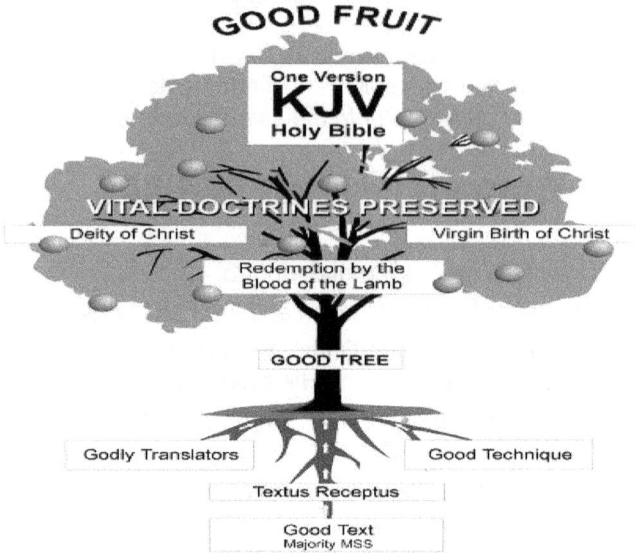

". . . every good tree bringeth forth good fruit."

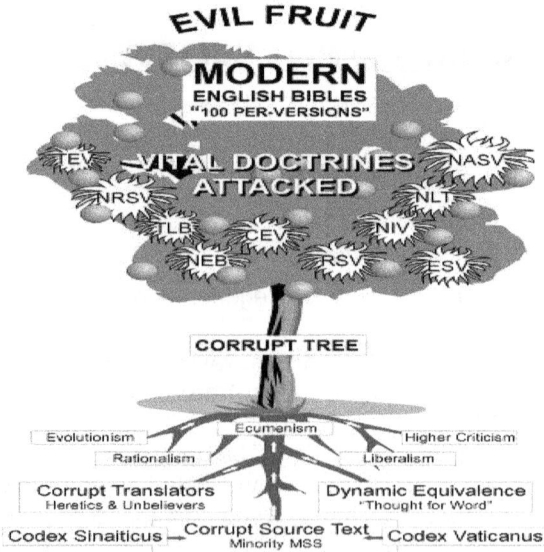

EVIL FRUIT

MODERN
ENGLISH BIBLES
"100 PER-VERSIONS"

VITAL DOCTRINES ATTACKED

TEV   NASV   NRSV   NLT   TLB   CEV   NIV   NEB   RSV   ESV

CORRUPT TREE

Ecumenism

Evolutionism

Higher Criticism

Rationalism

Liberalism

Corrupt Translators
Heretics & Unbelievers

Dynamic Equivalence
"Thought for Word"

Codex Sinaiticus

Corrupt Source Text
Minority MSS

Codex Vaticanus

". . . a corrupt tree bringeth forth evil fruit."

VI. THE TRANSLATORS' AWESOME TASK [8]

The translation of God's Word is an awesome task fraught with grave responsibility. What mortal being is worthy to handle and translate the words of the Almighty? Even as those who teach the Word of God must exercise utmost care: *...he word of the LORD was unto them precept upon precept, precept upon precept; line upon line, line upon line; here a little, and there a little..."* (Isa 28:13), so must they who translate God's Word exercise the utmost care.

Those who handle God's Word are warned: *"Every word of God is pure: . . . Add thou not unto his words, lest he reprove thee, and thou be found a liar"* (Prov 30:5–6). In repelling the tempter, our Lord used only God's Word, *"It is written, Man shall not live by bread alone, but by every word that proceedeth out of the mouth of God"* (Matt 4:4). **Every word in the Bible is important! Every word must be faithfully and precisely translated without distortion, without variation, whether more or less.**

Only with utmost reverence then should one handle God's Word. Such was the attitude of the men who translated the KJB. Those godly men of rare scholarship, holding a "high view" of Holy Scripture, endeavoured to translate **word for word** and **phrase for phrase** so as to capture the very spirit of the original text, and thus express the mind of God faithfully.

This precise "**word for word**" method ("formal equivalence" or "verbal equivalence") ensures that **the KJB conveys God's message with a degree of literal and grammatical fidelity unrivalled by any other modern English version.**

One Translator's Reckless Methodology

Eugene Nida is an unregenerate man who denies the blood atonement, the reality of angels and miracles, and the infallibility of Holy Scripture. Yet he occupied a key position in the Translations Department of the United Bible Societies.

By the introduction of his new translation methodology, "Dynamic Equivalence," Eugene Nida has become the most influential person in the field of Bible translation. The theory behind Nida's "Dynamic Equivalence" goes something like this:

a   The message and events of Scripture are bound in the culture of the past.

b   The strict "word for word" translation being "static" does not release the message of God.

c   "Dynamic Equivalence" unbinds the message which "leaps out" at the reader in today's language and culture.

d   By this method the translator is at liberty to express just **how he feels** were the Author's thoughts.

e   Instead of "**word for word**," it is now "**thought for word**," ie, man's thoughts in place of God's Word.

Eugene Nida's theory is theological **liberalism**, which is **unbelief**. It reduces God to man's level. It implies that God is unable to communicate with His creatures in an intelligible manner without man's aid.

Nida is an infidel, a "*corrupt tree*" which "*bringeth forth evil fruit*" (Matt 7:17).

The corrupted Modern English Bibles have come by the "Dynamic Equivalence" method of translation. A corrupt methodology gives rise to corrupt versions: "*by their fruits ye shall know them*" (Matt 7:20).

Heed the warning of the Scripture: "*For my thoughts are not your thoughts, neither are your ways my ways, saith the LORD*" (Isa 55:8). It is supreme folly and reckless presumption for any man to venture to "think God's thoughts" by wanton manipulation of God's inspired Word.

VII. THE DOCTOR'S PRESCRIPTION [9]

1.   A good doctor's prescription spells life and health to the patient. It is written in exact and precise terms. With **words** (and figures) the doctor expresses his **thoughts**.

2.   The doctor's prescription must not be tampered with: nothing must be added, nothing taken away. There must be no variation or manipulation.

3.   A good pharmacist dispenses the prescription exactly as written, **word for word, letter for letter**, precise to the minutest detail. Not even a "jot or tittle" must be altered. (A dot moved one space to the

right increases a dose tenfold!)

4. A good pharmacist dispenses good, wholesome, effective, healthful medicine. When taken, the patient recovers.

5. An enemy gets his hands on the prescription and alters it. A deadly medicine is dispensed. When taken, the patient dies.

Modern English Bibles are deadly medicine!

GOD'S WORD OUR PRESCRIPTION

1. Our God, the soul's Physician, has a Prescription for life: the Bible.

2. It comes to us by the hands of men of old inspired by the Holy Spirit, copyists, and translators. The business of these copyists and translators is to keep to the Bible text exactly as written: **word for word, letter for letter**, without alteration or variation.

3. The faithful "**word for word**" method of translation is termed "**Verbal Equivalence.**"

4. The translators of the **KJB Bible** appointed by King James used the **Verbal Equivalence** method, **word for word**, as originally given by God.

5. The **MSS** they used were faithful copies of the original, known as the *Received Text* (TR) or the *Majority Text*.

6. The result of their translation: a sound, accurate, faithful Bible, the "*King James Version*" or "*Authorized Version*" true to its Author in every vital detail.

7. We confidently believe that the **KJB** or **AV** is God's Word kept intact in English, God's perfect Prescription for the English-speaking world.

VIII. CONCLUSION

Our all-wise God has ordained that His purpose in Creation and Redemption should be accomplished by His Word. So highly has He esteemed His Word that He magnified it above His name (Ps 138:2). God's Word is forever settled in heaven (Ps 119:89); it cannot be broken (John 10:35), neither shall it pass away (Matt 24:35). Our Lord has confirmed, "*For verily I say unto you, Till heaven and earth pass, one jot or one tittle shall in no wise pass from the law, till all be fulfilled"* (Matt 5:18). Who, then, should dare to alter *"one jot or one tittle"* of the Word of God? Such reckless daring shall have its due reward: ... *"If any man shall add unto these things, God shall add unto him the plagues that are written in this book: And if any man shall take away from the words of the book of this prophecy, God shall take away his part out of the book of life..."* (Rev 22:18-19). God has spoken, be warned!

If we reject the doctrine of VPP, we effectively reject the faithful KJB as well. It is such an irony that VPP opponents who hold in high esteem the KJB and yet

(a) despise the KJB's underlying Hebrew and Greek texts, and

(b) believe that the preservation of the inspired Greek words of God is also to be found in the corrupt Westcott and Hort critical texts.

The battle today is the battle for the Bible. It is the battle for the King James Bible and its underlying Hebrew and Greek texts over the many modern English versions and their corrupt texts. This battle seeks to recapture for the Church the traditional text and the doctrine of Bible preservation.[10] God has certainly preserved His words for us today. But where are His words? They are the Hebrew words found in the Traditional Masoretic Hebrew Old Testament (Ben Chayyim) and the Greek words found in the Traditional Greek New Testament of Textus Receptus, the underlying original language texts of the King James Bible. The KJB accurately preserves the Hebrew and Greek words in the English language based on its four-fold superiority: Texts, Translators, Technique and Theology.

"When the enemy shall come in like a flood, the spirit of the LORD shall lift up a Standard against him" (Isa 59:19). *"... Thy Word is Truth"* (John 17:17). *"For we can do nothing against the Truth, but for the Truth"* (2 Cor 13:8). *"But the Word of the LORD endureth forever..."* (1 Pet 1:25). *"Nevertheless the Foundation of God standeth sure, having this seal, the Lord knoweth them that are His. And, Let every one that nameth the name of Christ depart from iniquity"* (2 Tim 2:19). Amen.

NOTES

[1] This part is adapted from chapter 1 of S H Tow's *In Defence of The King James Holy Bible*, a booklet published by Calvary Bible-Presbyterian Church, Singapore.

[2] This part is written with reference to D A Waite's *Defending The King James Bible* (Collingswood: The Bible For Today Press, 1994).

[3] Chapter 6 of *In Defence of the King James Holy Bible*.

[4] *The Divine Original* (London: Trinitarian Bible Society, nd), 6-7.

[5] David Cloud, *Modern Bible Versions* (Oak Harbor: Way of Life Literature, 1994), 28-30.

[6] Chapter 7 of *In Defence of the King James Holy Bible*.

[7] See D A Waite, *Heresies of Westcott and Hort* (Collingswood: The Bible For Today, 1979).

[8] Chapter 8 of *In Defence of the King James Holy Bible*.

[9] Ibid, chapter 9.

[10] Jeffrey Khoo, *Kept Pure In All Ages* (Singapore: Far Eastern Bible College Press, 2001), 17.

LESSON 8

Identification Of God's Preserved Words I

(TO BE CONTINUED IN THE NEXT LESSON 9)

Inspiration, Preservation, and Translations:
In Search of the Biblical Identity of the Bible-Presbyterian Church

I. THESIS

(1) The Holy Scriptures are verbally and plenarily inspired (VPI) by God in the original languages of Hebrew, Aramaic, and Greek.

(2) These VPI words in the original languages are verbally and plenarily preserved (VPP) by God throughout the ages, and found in the Hebrew Masoretic Text of the Old Testament and the Greek Textus Receptus of the New Testament.

(3) The King James or Authorized Version is a most faithful and reliable translation of these VPI and VPP Hebrew/Aramaic Old Testament and Greek New Testament words which are totally infallible and inerrant and hence supremely authoritative in all matters of faith and practice.

II. INSPIRATION

The Bible-Presbyterian (B-P) Constitution—Article 4.2.1—states,

We believe in the divine, verbal and plenary inspiration of the Scriptures in the original languages, their consequent inerrancy and infallibility, and as the Word of God, the Supreme and final authority in faith and life.

A. Definitions

Let us now define the important terms found in the above statement of faith.

The term, "divine, verbal and plenary inspiration" (VPI) means that the Holy Scriptures are a product of God's very own breath (2 Tim 3:16, *theopneustos*, literally "Godspiration" or "Godspired," and accurately rendered as "inspired of God" in the KJB) whereby God as Author supernaturally ensures that His inspired words as a whole (plenary) and in their parts to the last iota (verbal, cf Matt 4:4, 5:18) are not at all the words of sinful and fallible men but indeed the very words of the thrice holy and infallible God and thus entirely truthful and absolutely perfect, without any mistake or error (Ps 12:6, 19:7).

The divine VPI words are in the "original languages." What are the "original languages"? They are the Hebrew and Aramaic words of the Old Testament Scripture, and the Greek words of the New Testament Scripture.

The words "inerrancy and infallibility" tell us that the Holy Scriptures by virtue of its very nature as God's VPI words are without any mistake or error (inerrant), and incapable of error (infallible). The Bible is totally infallible and inerrant not only in matters of salvation, but also in matters of history, geography, and science.

The VPI Scripture being the very Word of God, infallible and inerrant, serves as the "Supreme and final authority" on all Christian beliefs and practices. In other words, what the Bible says rules and overrules all human theories and methods. God is always right, and man is wrong every time he disagrees with God (Rom 3:4). Every doctrine and practice of the church must be supported by the Scriptures and the Scriptures alone (not Scripture *plus* ...).

As such, Article 4.2.1 of the B-P Constitution is a fine statement of faith, and accurate on the 100% or perfect inspiration of the Bible not only as a whole (plenary inspiration) but down to its words (verbal inspiration) in the original languages of Hebrew, Aramaic, and Greek. The plain and natural reading of the statement assumes the present perfection of the Scriptures, that believers possess a 100% inspired Bible *in their hands* that is totally infallible and inerrant without any mistake and their sole and supreme authority of faith and practice.

B. Autographs Only or Apographs Also?

But in the present Bibliological crisis in the Singapore B-P Church, VPI as spelled out in Article 4.2.1 is interpreted by 11 pastors from 7 B-P churches (Galilee, Grace, Life, Nazareth, Olivet, Shalom, and Zion) to be applicable to the original "autographs" (ie, the very first scripts written by God Himself, or His prophets, or His apostles) without including the apographs (manuscript copies). They wrote saying, "*We ... wholeheartedly believe and affirm that the inspired Word of God has absolutely no error in the Original Autographs. However we reject ... Verbal Plenary Preservation.*" [1]

This "Autographs Only" view of infallibility and inerrancy is also held by the Board of Elders of Calvary B-P Church (Jurong) who in their paper on their "Non-VPP Stand" made their position very clear that "Only the original autographs of the OT and NT are the inspired, infallible and inerrant Word." [2]   Now it must be said that both evangelicals and fundamentalists affirm the VPI of the original autographs. There is therefore no issue here. This is also acknowledged in the Life B-P Church Sunday School paper of December 1, 2002 entitled, "Preserving Our Godly Path." In that paper it is clearly stated, "The debate concerning the "Perfect Bible" is NOT about the original writings (or the autographs) of the biblical writers (such as Moses, Peter or Paul)." We VPP advocates do not dispute the VPI of the autographs. The truth is VPP cannot stand without VPI and vice versa. Those who wish to preserve "godly paths" ought to realise that there will be no godly paths to preserve if God did not preserve His perfect words. *Perfect Bible first before godly paths* is theologically correct.

So what is the issue all about if it is not about VPI? The issue is all about this: Is the Word of God infallible and inerrant in the autographs and the *autographs only*, or is the Word of God infallible and inerrant in the *apographs also*? Simply asked: Is the Word of God perfect only in the past but no longer perfect today? Is the Bible of today a lost and broken relic or is it a precise and exact representation of the Original that God gave in the beginning by virtue of His perfect preservation of every jot and tittle of His inspired words in the Original?

Anti-VPPists argue from Article 4.2.1 of the B-P Constitution that the infallible and inerrant Scriptures are *only in the autographs*. But where does it say so? Nowhere! It must be underscored that it stands precisely written in Article 4.2.1 that the inspired Scriptures the B-P Church believes to be infallible and inerrant are the Scriptures in the "*original languages*" and not simply and only the autographs. Why do the 11 pastors alter the sense of the Constitution by interpreting the word "languages" to mean "autographs" if not to exclude what they consider as "theory" but what we see as "doctrine" that the Bible is presently infallible and inerrant?

Now if what the anti-VPPists say is true that the perfect and authoritative Scriptures can refer only to the autographs, then *where are the autographs*? Do they not agree that the autographs have already perished and are no more? And if so where are the fully inspired, totally inerrant, and absolutely authoritative Scriptures that Bible believers can use confidently and declare, "Thus saith the Lord"? If we only believe that God has only inspired but did not preserve His words, we will not be able to say we have God's totally infallible, inerrant and supremely authoritative Word today.

Now, if we do indeed have the inspired words of God today, then where are they? This brings us to the divine and special providential preservation of the Holy Scriptures.

III. PRESERVATION

Do we have the inspired words of God today in the *original languages* (Hebrew, Aramaic, and Greek)? If we do, then where are they? That is the key question which the "autographs alone" advocates cannot answer. They confess that the autographs are long gone and no more. As such, how can a non-existent authority serve as our final authority? An authority must be existent, tangible, available right now, at this time, or else it can be no authority at all. It goes without saying that an appeal to the non-existent autographs as the Church's supreme and final authority is both illogical and untenable.

The veracity and validity of the Biblical Covenant is undermined when the 11 pastors affirm VPI but not VPP. They confidently affirm the total infallibility and inerrancy of the non-existent autographs (which they do not have and cannot produce), but cannot believe in a verbally and plenarily preserved and hence presently existing infallible and inerrant Scripture in the original languages (which they pejoratively call a "theory" and a "new doctrine"). They wrote dismissively, "we reject the theory of Verbal Plenary Preservation ... that the Greek and Hebrew copies immediately underlying the King James Version are an exact replica of the Original Autographs." Note that they have no biblical basis whatsoever for their non-VPP position. It is purely their opinion, or may I also say only a "theory"? But by the logic of faith, we VPP believers declare that we indeed have God's infallible and inerrant Word in our hands today, and identify the inspired Hebrew, Aramaic, and Greek words behind the King James Bible to be precisely the words God has perfectly preserved.

A. Imperfect Hebrew and Greek Texts?

In a Life B-P Church "Statement of Clarification," issued on January 19, 2003, the majority of the session (2 assistant pastors, 4 elders, and 12 deacons) and three preachers opposed their founding pastor—Rev Dr Timothy Tow—who affirmed the Bible to be "100% perfect without any mistake." In their "Statement of Clarification" they wrote, "While agreeing wholeheartedly to the KJB Bible being the very Word of God and fully reliable, **the contributors of 'Preserving Our Godly Path' paper do not believe that the Hebrew and Greek texts that underlie the KJB are perfect**" (emphasis in the original). Question: How can they endorse the KJB as "the very (ie, complete, absolute, utter) Word of God and fully reliable" and yet "not believe that the Hebrew and Greek texts that underlie the KJB are perfect" (ie, complete, flawless, exact)? How can the KJB—a translation—be 100% without its source texts—the Hebrew and Greek Scriptures—being 100%? This is highly illogical and unnatural. As Jesus said, "For a good tree bringeth not forth corrupt fruit; neither doth a corrupt tree bring forth good fruit" (Luke 6:43).

Unlike non-VPP KJB users who say yes to the KJB but no to the Hebrew, Aramaic, and Greek words underlying the KJB, VPP advocates say yes to the KJB and yes also to the Hebrew, Aramaic, and Greek words behind the KJB. We believe the KJB to be the Word of God precisely because the Hebrew, Aramaic, and Greek words underlying it are the very words God has inspired and preserved, and therefore 100% perfect, without any mistake. We say yes to the KJB, and a double yes to the original language Scriptures behind the KJB. Is this not biblically logical and consistent? Does it not instill faith and confidence in God and His Word for B-Ps who have always used and trusted the KJB as God's Word?[3]

B. Lost Words?

The 11 B-P pastors' rejection of VPP surely contradicts the Westminster Confession of Faith (WCF) to which every Reformed or Presbyterian Church (and certainly the B-P Church) subscribes. It is significant to note that the WCF speaks of the authenticity of the

Scriptures in terms of the *original language* Scriptures, namely the "Old Testament *in Hebrew*" and the "New Testament *in Greek*" (note the absence of the "autographs" in the Confession). Chapter I and paragraph VIII of the WCF states,

> The Old Testament in Hebrew (which was the native language of the people of God of old), and the New Testament in Greek (which at the time of the writing of it, was most generally known to the nations), being immediately inspired by God, and, by *His singular care and providence, kept pure in all ages,* are therefore authentic; so as, in all controversies of religion, the Church is finally to appeal unto them.

The affirmation "by His singular care and providence" clearly states that Biblical preservation is *God's work* and not man's. That is why this providence is a *special* one. That is why it has to be verbal and not just doctrinal preservation. If God is the One who single-handedly preserves His inspired words and keeps them pure, we can expect Him to do no less than a perfect job—*every word is kept intact and none is lost.* For biblical support, the Westminster theologians cited Matthew 5:18, "For verily I say unto you, Till heaven and earth pass, one jot or one tittle shall in no wise pass from the law, till all be fulfilled." Does not the declaration that the Holy Scriptures are truly and presently "authentical" (ie, perfect, genuine, true) because they have been kept pure "by His singular care and providence" mean precisely "the divine, verbal and plenary preservation" of the Scriptures? How can God's preservation of His inspired words in the Holy Scriptures be less than infallible, entire, total, complete, and full? But anti-VPPists speak of only "essential" (ie, partial) preservation—the doctrines, truths, claims are preserved (ie, conceptual or thought preservation), not the words (ie, verbal preservation) for in their judgment some words of Scripture have been lost and are no more (eg, 1 Sam 13:1, 2 Chron 22:2). They then assure us that in their scholarly opinion, these lost words of Scripture are unnecessary for our faith and will not affect our salvation because they are "redundant" and "insignificant." Does this "lost Bible" or "lost words" view of preservation not contradict God's own promise of jot-and-tittle preservation in Matthew 5:18 as cited by the Westminster divines?

C. Jot-and-Tittle Preservation

This anti-VPP "lost words" view does indeed contradict the promissory words of Jesus. How do anti-VPPists respond? They respond by saying, "We must reexamine what Jesus said in Matthew 5:18. Perhaps 'jot and tittle' does not mean literally 'jot and tittle', but is an exaggeration." Is this what they mean by a "godly path" to God and His Word? In "preserving our godly path" should we not reexamine our ignorant selves and our fallible thoughts instead? Should we not apply the infallible principle of the glory of God in our regard for our Lord and the interpretation of His Word (Isa 42:8, Jer 9:23-24, John 7:18)? Should we not take God's Word literally unless it is clearly figurative? Surely God says what He means and means what He says. "God says it, that settles it, and we believe it." This has always been the basic hermeneutical ethos of Biblical fundamentalists and inerrantists. Does not puny man know that the almighty God has magnified His Word above all His Name (Ps 138:2)?

It is crucial to know that the Reformers never thought of the perfection or infallibility of the Scriptures only in terms of the non-existent autographs but always in terms of the ever-existing apographs. According to Richard Muller,

> The Protestant scholastics do not press the point made by their nineteenth-century followers that the infallibility of Scripture and the freedom of Scripture from error reside absolutely in the *autographa* and only in a derivative sense in the *apographa*; rather, the scholastics argue positively that the *apographa* preserve intact the true words of the prophets and the apostles and that the God-breathed (*theopneustos*) character of Scripture is manifest in the *apographa* as well as in the *autographa*. [4]

The Westminster divines in 1648 believed their Bible to be totally infallible and inerrant without any mistake. This is observed by William Orr who wrote,

> Now this affirms that the Hebrew text of the Old Testament and the Greek of the New which was known to the Westminster divines was immediately inspired by God because it was *identical* with the first text that God has kept pure in all the ages. *The idea that there are mistakes in the Hebrew Masoretic texts or in the Textus Receptus of the New Testament was unknown to the authors of the Confession of Faith.* [5]

Which Hebrew OT text and Greek NT text did the Westminster divines use in their day? Was it not the Hebrew Masoretic Text and the Greek Textus Receptus that underlie the Reformation Bibles as best represented by the KJB? If the Westminster pastors and theologians did not think that the Bible they possessed in their day had any mistake, why is it so wrong and sinful for us today to also believe that the same Hebrew and Greek Scriptures the Westminster divines used are without any mistake?

IV. VPI WITHOUT VPP IS USELESS

The question however remains: Does Article 4.2.1 deny the biblical doctrine of the 100% preservation of the inspired words in the original languages? It is obvious that the B-P Constitution in keeping to the Westminster Confession of Faith and the Biblical doctrine of the infallibility and inerrancy of Scriptures wrote the words "original languages" and not "Original Autographs" for the Scriptures in the "original languages" apply not only to the autographs but also the apographs without which we have no infallible and inerrant Scriptures today to serve as our final and supreme authority of faith and practice. Although it may be argued that it is inspiration and not preservation of the Scriptures that is mentioned in Article 4.2.1, preservation is surely implied and only logical for why would God want to inspire a perfect Bible in the beginning without wanting to preserve it? Will a person apply hair tonic to his head if he wants to be bald?

Myron Houghton of Faith Baptist Seminary, though not a Textus Receptus or KJB man, was nonetheless honest and truthful in this observation of his,

> "All Scripture is given by inspiration of God" [2 Timothy 3:16]. Another way of saying this would be, "all Scripture is God-breathed," or "all Scripture comes from the mouth of God." This means God is directly responsible for causing the Bible writers to put down everything that He wanted written without error and without omission. But what of the Bible I hold in my hand? Is it God's Word? Can it be trusted? The answer is yes! Both truths—the inspiration and inerrancy of the original manuscripts and the trustworthiness of the Bible in my hand—must be acknowledged. To affirm the inspiration and inerrancy of the original writings while casting doubt on the authority of the Bible that is available to us is just plain silly. Can you really imagine someone seriously saying, "I have good news and I have bad news: the good news is that God wanted to give us a message and therefore caused a book to be written; the bad news is that He didn't possess the power to preserve it and therefore we don't know what it said!" A view of

inspiration without a corresponding view of preservation is of no value.[6]

Ian Paisley, renowned leader of the World Congress of Fundamentalists and an ardent defender of the KJB and its underlying texts, observed likewise:

> "The verbal Inspiration of the Scriptures demands the verbal Preservation of the Scriptures. Those who would deny the need for verbal Preservation cannot be accepted as being really committed to verbal Inspiration. If there is no preserved Word of God today then the work of Divine Revelation and Divine Inspiration has perished." [7]

V. PRESERVATION: THE BRIDGE BETWEEN INSPIRATION AND TRANSLATION

But it is sad that those who are expected to champion the verbal inspiration of Scripture are so quick to deny its verbal preservation. Such a denial of VPP is seen in a statement issued on October 29, 2005 by the Singapore Council of Christian Churches (SCCC) entitled "The Inspiration and Translations of the Holy Scriptures":

> Recently some brethren in Singapore have been advocating that apart from the verbal plenary inspiration (VPI) and consequent inerrancy and infallibility of The Scriptures in the original languages, the Hebrew Masoretic Text and the Greek Textus Receptus manuscripts immediately underlying the King James Version are also verbally and plenarily preserved being an exact replica of the Original Autographs. This Verbal Plenary Preservation (VPP) theory for the KJB's underlying texts thus claiming "100% perfection" for the KJB, is without Biblical foundation. This has not been, and is not the position of the ICCC or SCCC or other ICCC-affiliated organizations. The SCCC therefore calls upon its members and all other Bible-believing brethren not to subscribe to this new, Biblically unfounded and unproven theory.[8]

The question I would like to ask is: Why did they not entitle their statement, "The Inspiration, *Preservation*, and Translations of the Holy Scriptures"? Why is there no "Preservation"? Without preservation, what is the use of inspiration? Without preservation how can there be translations? The fallacy of the SCCC statement is precisely due to this "missing link" which is "Preservation." Notwithstanding the missing link of "Preservation," the SCCC statement in its published form saw a quick "evolution." The November-December 2005 issue of the *Far Eastern Beacon* published an "improved" version of its primitive forebear passed on October 29, 2005. Here is a comparison of the old and new statements of the SCCC against VPP:

> Recently some brethren in Singapore <u>and elsewhere</u> have been ~~advocating~~<u>promulgating</u> that apart from the verbal plenary inspiration (VPI) and <u>the</u> consequent inerrancy and infallibility of ~~The~~<u>the</u> Holy Scriptures in the original languages,~~ the Hebrew Masoretic Text and the Greek Textus Receptus manuscripts immediately underlying the King James Version are also verbally and plenarily~~ <u>of Hebrew, Aramaic, and Greek, "the words of the Received Greek and Masoretic Hebrew texts that underlie the King James Bible are the very words which God has</u> preserved <u>down through the centuries</u> being ~~an~~<u>the</u> exact ~~replica~~<u>words</u> of the ~~Original Autographs~~<u>originals themselves"</u>. This <u>theory of claiming</u> Verbal Plenary Preservation (VPP) ~~theory~~ <u>for the KJB's underlying texts</u> ~~thus claiming "100% perfection" for the KJB~~<u>and their exact identification with the Holy Scriptures in the original languages</u>, is without Biblical foundation. This has not been, and is not the position of the ICCC or SCCC or other ICCC-affiliated organizations. The SCCC therefore calls upon its members and all other Bible-believing brethren not to subscribe to this new, Biblically unfounded and unproven theory.

The revised version continues to deny VPP. Many today believe in inspiration and translation but not preservation. Such a belief begs the question: How could the inspired autographs serve as the basis for any translation if they have not been preserved by God? *Without preservation there is just a great chasm with no bridge to cross from inspiration to translation.* Despite our many attempts to define and clarify what VPP means, and why this doctrine is vital for the protection of the Christian Faith, the safeguarding of the beloved KJB (which the SCCC claims to uphold), and the basis for faithful translations of the Scriptures into other languages, the SCCC remains insistent on denying VPP, even pugnacious in pushing for its rejection.

VI. VPP IS HONOURABLE NOT HERETICAL

In Calvary Jurong's "Non-VPP" paper, it is stated that the "ICCC (SCCC) calls on all Christians not to accept the VPP teaching."[9] When did the ICCC pass a resolution against VPP or endorse the SCCC statement against VPP? What the ICCC did do however under Carl McIntire's presidency was to pass an excellent resolution not only in Amsterdam in 1997 but also in Jerusalem in 2000 affirming the superiority of the KJB over against the modern versions, and the Bible to be "Forever Infallible and Inerrant" with the following fine declaration of faith:

The O.T. has been preserved in the Masoretic text and the N.T. in the Textus Receptus, combined they gave us the complete Word of God. The King James Version in English has been faithfully translated from these God-preserved manuscripts.[10]

The ICCC clearly resolved to uphold the "forever infallible and inerrant" Scriptures which is nothing short of VPP, and identified the complete and preserved Scriptures to be the Hebrew Masoretic Text and the Greek Textus Receptus from which the KJB has been faithfully translated. This is precisely the stand taken by FEBC and all VPP advocates. It goes without saying that the SCCC has seriously undermined the credibility of the ICCC by such an act against VPP, and the inspired and preserved Hebrew, Aramaic, and Greek words underlying the KJB. It even "calls upon its members and all other Bible-believing brethren not to subscribe to this new, Biblically unfounded and unproven theory." Is it not strange for the SCCC to call on "Bible-believing" brethren to believe that the Bible they have in their hands today contains mistakes? What kind of "Bible-believing" faith is this? If the SCCC disagrees with but does not discriminate against VPP, that would not be unreasonable, but they intend to ban and silence VPP which is not only unfair but also unjust. Is this not an attempt at schism?

The SCCC (echoing the group of 11 pastors) claims that the "promulgation" of VPP is "schismatic." Not so. *It is not the promulgation but the prohibition and persecution of VPP that is schismatic.* The anti-VPPists can go ahead to preach and write that the Bible is no longer infallible and inerrant since in their mind it contains some insignificant mistakes (whether God is pleased or grieved by this, and whether His people will accept it or be stumbled, should be left to the convicting work and judgement of the Holy Spirit in the hearts of His saints); but why should they forbid and prevent VPP believers from declaring and defending the Bible they have in their hands today to be truly infallible and inerrant without any mistake?

If anti-VPPists feel that they cannot know whether the inspired words of God are perfectly preserved today, then they should be chagrined, but why cannot they rejoice with those who by faith are certain they have all of God's inspired words and know exactly where all the inspired words are preserved—in the Hebrew, Aramaic, and Greek Scriptures underlying the KJB? Peter Masters of Spurgeon's Tabernacle though not in total agreement with our position on VPP was at least honest enough to acknowledge that our position is an "*honourable*" one[11] unlike those anti-VPPists who maliciously label it "foolish," "extreme," "schismatic," "heretical," "cultic," and even "Roman Catholic"!

VII. TRANSLATIONS

Not everyone today can read the Scriptures in the original languages. There is thus a need for the Scriptures to be translated into the common language of the people. The WCF shares this concern for the Bible to be translated,

> But, because these original tongues are not known to all the people of God, who have right unto, and interest in the Scriptures, and are commanded, in the fear of God, to read and search them, therefore they are to be translated into the vulgar language of every nation unto which they come, that, the Word of God dwelling plentifully in all, they may worship Him in an acceptable manner; and, through patience and comfort of the Scriptures, may have hope (I:VIII).

By the grace of God, the Hebrew and Greek Scriptures have been translated into many languages of the world. Insofar as the English translation is concerned, we are thankful to the Lord for the KJB, the best of all the good old versions of the Protestant Reformation. Today the KJB is being challenged by the many modern versions that seek to usurp its rightful place as the only English version that can rightly be called "the very Word of God." D A Waite, President of the Dean Burgon Society, has given four reasons why the KJB is superior to all the other English translations available in the world today. In his ground-breaking book, *Defending the King James Bible: A Fourfold*

Superiority, he argued that the KJB is superior in terms of its (1) Texts, (2) Translators, (3) Technique, and (4) Theology[12]. Even non-fundamentalists are hailing the goodness of this grand old version in terms of its translational accuracy and literary beauty.[13] The KJB was not only a translation that transformed a nation; it was *the* translation that transformed the world *literarily* speaking.[14]

A. Perfectly Flawless Translation?

At this juncture, let me deal with Calvary Jurong's report on what the Rev Charles Seet wrote concerning my response to Gary Hudson's "Questions for the KJB-Only Cult." Calvary Jurong's report is skewed in such a way as to make me look like (1) I am defending a "perfectly flawless Bible translation" (underlining in the original), and (2) I believe that there was "no Word of God prior to 1611."[15] The account totally left out my lengthy answer to Gary Hudson's question. Without giving the proper context, it thus misleads the reader. Allow me to produce in full my answer so that the reader may judge for himself whether Calvary Jurong has or has not represented me correctly in its "Non-VPP" paper.

> **(1) Must we possess a perfectly flawless Bible translation in order to call it "the word of God"? If so, how do we know "it" is perfect? If not, why do some limit "the word of God" to only one 17th Century English translation? Where was "the word of God" prior to 1611?** [Note: This was Gary Hudson's question, and not Charles Seet's questioning of me as painted out in the Calvary Jurong report thereby making me look like a Ruckmanite.]
>
> [Answer] We believe that "the King James Version (or Authorized Version) of the English Bible is a true, faithful, and accurate translation of these two providentially preserved Texts [Traditional Masoretic Hebrew Text and Traditional Greek Text underlying the KJB], which in our time has no equal among all of the other English Translations. The translators did such a fine job in their translation task that we can without apology hold up the Authorized Version and say 'This is the Word of God!' while at the same time realizing that, in some verses, we must go back to the underlying original language Texts for complete clarity, and also compare Scripture with Scripture." (*The Dean Burgon Society, "Articles of Faith," section II.A.*)

Every Bible translation can be legitimately called the Word of God if it is true and faithful to the original and traditional text. We refuse to consider heretical Bibles like the New World Translation of the Jehovah's Witnesses as "the Word of God." We also reject as unreliable all Bible versions (eg NIV, TEV, TLB, CEV ...) that are a result of the dynamic equivalence method of translation, and those (eg RSV, NASB, ESV ...) that cast doubt and/or omit verses based on corrupted readings of the Alexandrian or Westcott-Hort Text, and consider them unsafe for use.

Where was the Word of God prior to 1611? Well, the Word of God is found in the divinely inspired and providentially preserved Traditional and Preserved Text of OT and NT Scriptures used and recognized by the Church down through the ages, and in all the faithful and reliable translations that were based on those Texts, viz, Martin Luther's German Bible (1522), William Tyndale's Bible (1525), Myles Coverdale's Bible (1535), The Matthew's Bible (1537), The Great Bible (1539-41), and The Geneva Bible (1557-60).

It is significant to note that prior to the KJB, the English translations were largely individual efforts. The KJB on the other hand is a corporate work. In the words of the translators, the KJB was not produced "to make a bad one a good one; but to make a good one better, or out of many good ones one principal good one." For this purpose and with such devotion the KJB translation committee was formed, and they were careful to "assemble together; not too many, lest one should trouble another; and yet many, lest many things haply might escape them."

The King James Bible is a product of the 16th Century Protestant Reformation. The providential hand of God was clearly at work at the time of the Reformation not only in the separation of the true church from the false church, but also in the invention of the printing press, the renewed interest in the study of the original languages, the publication of the Textus Receptus which finally culminated in the translation of the KJB. These products of the Protestant Reformation bear the divine imprimatur.

God holds His people in every age responsible for using the divinely inspired and preserved original texts and only the faithful and accurate translations of His Word. The KJB-only position (not

Ruckmanism) does not limit the Word of God to only one 17th Century English Translation, but advocates that the KJB, being still the most accurate English translation based on the purest texts, should be the only Bible used by English-speaking Christians today. To use other Bibles when the best is clearly available would be to neglect our responsibility.[16]

Can the pastor and the elders of Calvary Jurong who object to my defense of the KJB kindly let me know which part of the above answer is not in line with the B-P stand on the KJB? Now the Rev Seet might possibly take issue with the word "purest" (meaning the best, without any mistake) to refer to the underlying texts of the KJB, for he believes that they are only "closest" (since he considers the underlying texts to contain "scribal errors" especially in places where there are absolutely none, eg, 2 Chron 22:2).[17] It needs to be made known that I have no qualms with the word "closest" if it is taken to mean that (1) the Bible is entirely (100%) preserved and not just essentially (99.9%) preserved, (2) the Bible is verbally preserved and not just conceptually preserved, and (3) the Bible is indeed infallible and inerrant not just in the past but also today. But they speak adversely of those who take the Dean Burgon Oath,[18] who believe that the Bible they have in their hands today have (1) no lost words and (2) no mistakes not only in its saving truths, but also in its numbers, names, dates, and places. Insofar as English versions are concerned, **the KJB is the closest to the purest Bible in the original languages that our all-powerful God has supernaturally preserved and His Spirit-indwelt Church has faithfully received throughout the ages**.

B. Perfect in the Original Languages

Since the Rev Seet has allowed his personal correspondence with me to go public,[19] allow me then to share my email of June 27, 2002, written in reply to his concerns about why I switched from addressing a so-called "perfectly flawless translation" (Hudson's caricature) to a perfectly flawless text in the original languages (ie, the Hebrew, Aramaic and Greek words underlying the KJB):[20]

[Charles Seet] **"1) I think some may take issue with the wording of the first paragraph,[21] as it implies that the texts underlying the KJB translation are not only closest to the original (as stated in our positional statement) but they are in fact virtual photocopies of the autographs, since the word 'flawless' means 'without defect'. Actually the first paragraph**

misses the point of the question, which is about 'perfectly flawless Bible translation' (not text).'

[My Reply] Yes, I am quite aware of this (viz, that the [ie, Hudson's] question had to do with translation not text). I did not want to be drawn into Hudson's trap and fallacious reasoning. That is why I redefined the question and redrew the rules of engagement. I wanted to state our understanding of the text at the outset before going on to address the matter of translation which I did in my 2nd paragraph.

You are also correct to conclude that my statement meant that the texts underlying the KJB may be considered "virtual photocopies of the autographs." The word "closest" as used in our position statement quoting the Dean Burgon Society should not be taken to mean that we only have a 99% pure text (1% error). I believe God has inspired and preserved His Word and words 100%. I can see how some may understand the word "closest" to mean "not perfect or exactly the same," ie, we may have most of or essentially God's words, but not all of God's words in the texts underlying our KJB. I think we need to understand the context in which the statement was phrased. Westcott and Hort puffed up their cut-up Greek text as being "closest to the original" since they based it on the 4th century Alexandrian manuscripts, which manuscripts Dean Burgon has dismissed as "most corrupt." Our use of the term "closest" seeks to *correct and counteract* Westcott and Hort's view on the identity of the true text. The term "closest" also distinguishes between the autograph (past and "lost") and the apograph (present and existing). We do not deny that the autograph and apograph *though distinct are the same*. The paper may be different, but the *contents* are the same.

Would the Rev Seet now kindly let me know in what way was my reply to him in defense of the KJB "heretical"? It was quite clear to him from the outset that I was not addressing a "perfectly flawless translation" but a "perfectly flawless text." Knowing this, why is he giving people the impression that I am actually talking about a "perfectly flawless translation"? The **LIE** is spread that Jeffrey Khoo believes in "post-canonical inspiration"—that "the KJB was given by inspiration." Why such deceit?

Another thing that baffles me is why the Rev Seet who claims to be strongly supportive of the KJB against the modern versions would launch such a campaign against VPP which is a precious biblical doctrine that actually protects and preserves the KJB? Why is all this done despite his assurance in 2004 that VPP should not be discriminated against? Why does he call me "extreme" if there should be no discrimination? Why is he and his supporters trying to silence VPP which safeguards the KJB which is the official Bible of the B-P Church since its founding? Why are anti-VPP/KJB men from BJU allowed to speak at his pulpit, but a ban is placed on certain B-P pastors who are VPP/KJB-defenders, even calling them "extreme" and "schismatic"? Why are enemies of the KJB promoted, but friends of the KJB cut down?

VIII. INSPIRATION, PRESERVATION, TRANSLATIONS: FOUR VIEWS

Is the B-P Church's stand on the KJB a matter of "preference" or a matter of "principle or doctrine"? We believe our use of the KJB and our defence of its underlying original language texts (words) is a matter of principle or doctrine. As a matter of principle or doctrine, our KJB defence is not based on convenience but conviction. There are four views on the issue of inspiration, preservation, and translations. Of course, there are different shades of views in between, but which view is the biblically acceptable view?

VIEW QUESTION	Rationalistic[22] (Liberal)	Eclectic[23] (Neo- Evangelical)	Deistic[24] (Neo- Fundamental)	Fideistic[25] (Reformed & Fundamental)
Inspiration 100% VPI?	No	Yes & No	Yes	Yes
Preservation 100% VPP?	No	No	No	Yes
Infallibility & Inerrancy?	Nowhere	Autographs only/ partially	Autographs only	Autographs & Apographs
Bible Today?	Imperfect	Imperfect	Imperfect	Perfect
Biblical Basis?	No	No	No	Yes (eg. Matt 5:18)
What Preserved?	Nothing	Doctrines not words	Doctrines not words	Words & doctrines
Words Lost?	Yes	Yes	Yes	No
Discrepancies in Bible (eg. 2 Chron	Yes	Yes	Yes	No

22:2)?				
Westcott & Hort?	For	For	Neither for nor against	Against
English Version?	RSV/NRSV & mordernistic versions only	NIV & modern versions mainly	NKJB & NASV mainly	Only KJB[26]

Which position ought we to take as B-Ps? Biblically and historically, we have taken the fideistic (faith) position which is the Reformed and Fundamentalist position on Biblical inspiration and preservation, and the KJB as the *best* translation of the English Bible: "So then faith cometh by hearing and hearing by the Word of God" (Rom 10:17). Only the faith position has any biblical basis resting on Psalm 12:6-7, Matthew 5:18, 24:35, John 10:35, 1 Peter 1:25, and many other passages.[27] The various anti- or non-VPP positions have no biblical support whatsoever.

Regardless of the absence of biblical support for their non-VPP stance which is based on non-Scriptural and subjectively interpreted "evidence," certain ones have accused FEBC of changing the doctrinal stand of the B-P Church on the Bible and the KJB. If a person would take a step back and look at the whole controversy objectively, he will see that FEBC is actually strengthening and not changing the original KJB position of the B-P Church. The B-P Church has always used the KJB as the Word of God from the beginning. Our KJB position is strengthened by the doctrine of VPP which argues for the 100% purity of the Hebrew and Greek Scriptures underlying the KJB over against the corrupt Westcott and Hort texts behind the modern English versions which are filled with errors.

Who better to speak for the B-P faith than the founder of the Singapore B-P movement and FEBC himself—the Rev Dr Timothy Tow—who believes without equivocation "the special providential preservation of Scripture," and "a 100% perfect Bible without any mistake"[28]? Rev Dr Timothy Tow—the only theologian at the founding of the B-P movement—is supported by Dr S H Tow—founding leader of the B-P Church in Singapore and senior pastor of the Calvary churches—who believes likewise, and has identified for us where precisely this "100% perfect Bible without any mistake" is:

1.   Question: Can we identify these texts?

2.   Answer: Absolutely. Our great God did not leave Himself without witness, but preserved perfectly a body of MSS: the Masoretic Hebrew Old Testament Text and the Received Greek New Testament Text (Textus Receptus). From these perfectly preserved copies of God's inspired, inerrant, infallible Scriptures, is derived our KJB.

3.   What is "VPP"? "V" is "Verbal," meaning "word for word" (Websters Dictionary). "P" is "Plenary," meaning "complete or absolute" (Websters Dictionary). "P" is "Preservation" meaning "kept from corruption or error."

4.   "VPP of Scripture" refers to the supernatural and special providential care of God over the ages (Westminster Confession of Faith Chapter I, VIII; see also Ps 12:6,7; Matt 5:18, 24:35; 1 Pet 1:25), safeguarding the transmission of the MSS by scribes or copyists, so that the body of texts (Masoretic Hebrew OT and Received Greek NT) have been kept pure as the "good tree" giving us the "good fruit," the KJB.

5.   As the attacks on God's Word increase in intensity, God's faithful remnant people also increase and intensify in their loyalty to God's Word without which the Gospel's entire foundation would collapse.

6.   The inspired and preserved Word of God for the Bible-Presbyterian Church is upheld by a "threefold cord" which cannot be broken, namely: (i) Constitution 4.2.1, (ii) the VPP of God's Word, (iii) the KJB, the Reformation Bible.29

Dr S H Tow went on to issue this pertinent warning:

Mark these words: The present attack on the VPP will lead ultimately to a denial and betrayal of the KJB. This is a prediction worth watching. God bless all readers with spiritual discernment.[30]

Having discussed the Biblical identity of the B-P Church as regards Inspiration, Preservation, and Translations, our next part will concentrate on the identification of the preserved words of the Hebrew OT and Greek NT underlying the KJB, with special attention on specific words of Scripture that are currently under attack by certain anti-KJB and non-VPP authors who call themselves "fundamentalists." Part II is entitled, "Canon, Texts, and Words: Lost and Found or Preserved and Identified?"

NOTES

[1] "A Statement on the Theory of Verbal Plenary Preservation (VPP)," Life Bible-Presbyterian Weekly, September 25, 2005.

[2] "Explanation of Our Non-VPP Stand," presented on Sunday, November 6, 2005 to the congregation of Calvary Jurong B-P Church by Rev James Chan Lay Seng, Pastor of Calvary Jurong B-P Church.

[3] *At this juncture, it needs to be made known that prior to putting forth his name as a subscriber to the "Statement of Clarification" in which the subscribers agree that the KJB is the "very Word of God and fully reliable," the Rev Charles Seet in August 2002 wrote an article—"How I Understand the Preservation of the Word of God"—to point out what he considers to be translational errors in certain parts of the English KJB.*

[4] *Dictionary of Latin and Greek Theological Terms,* sv "autographa" (emphasis mine).

[5] William F Orr, "The Authority of the Bible as Reflected in the Proposed Confession of 1967," as quoted by Letis, The Majority Text, 174 (emphasis mine).

[6] Myron J Houghton, "The Preservation of Scripture," *Faith Pulpit* (August 1999): 1-2.

[7] Ian R K Paisley, *My Plea for the Old Sword* (Belfast: Ambassador, 1997), 103.

[8] *Inspiration and Translations of the Holy Scriptures," a resolution passed by the Singapore Council of Christian Churches (SCCC), at its 49th AGM on Octrober 29, 2005 held at Life B-P Church, Singapore.*

[9] "Explanation of Our Non-VPP Stand," 13.

[10] Jeffrey Khoo, *Kept Pure in All Ages* (Singapore: FEBC Press, 2001), 125-6. The ICCC resolution was originally published in the Far Eastern Beacon.

[11.] It is reported in the October 2, 2005 True Life B-P Church Weekly (ed Timothy Tow) that Dr Peter Masters "did not think our VPP position to be in any way 'heretical,' but indeed *an honourable one.*' He also gave unreserved support and endorsement of FEBC, *'May I say that the ministry of FEBC under Dr Timothy Tow ... is a remarkable manifestation of the blessing of God in maintaining inerrancy, fundamentals, evangelism, sound hermeneutics and biblical separation. Your work is magnificent and encouraging in the highest degree.'* In another letter, Dr Masters reaffirmed his remarks on the VPP of Scripture that *'it is a sincerely held view aimed at safeguarding the Word, and promoting integrity. Its advocates seek to proclaim and adhere to the Gospel and the historic doctrines of the faith. They seek to preserve an excellent translation of the Bible, and to oppose the corrupt W & H based translations ... the position is honourable. It is certainly not base, self-seeking, unfaithful, or heretical in the sense of denying any doctrine of the Christian faith.'"*

[12.] D A Waite, *Defending the King James Bible*, 2nd ed (Collingswood: Bible For Today, 1996).

[13] For example, Leland Ryken wrote, "The KJB is the greatest English Bible translation ever produced. Its style combines simplicity and majesty as the original requires, though it inclines toward the exalted. Its rhythms are matchless." *The Word of God in English* (Wheaton: Crossway, 2002), 51.

[14] See Alister McGrath, *In the Beginning: The Story of the King James Bible* (London: Hodder and Stoughton, 2001).

[15] "Explanation of Our Non-VPP Stand," 2.

[16] "KJB Q&A," July 31, 2002 draft [words in square brackets not in original]. It is no secret that the Rev Charles Seet together with Rev Colin Wong declared that they could no longer take the Dean Burgon Oath in the FEBC faculty meeting of October 29, 2002. Rev Seet handed in his resignation letter to FEBC on November 15, 2002. In it he requested "not to be represented as a member of the FEBC faculty in any publication that is issued by the college from now on." I respect his decision, and take full responsibility for all that I have written in defence of the KJB and its underlying texts. Rev Seet has every freedom to disagree with me, but he and his friends have no right to misrepresent and malign me and those at FEBC who defend the KJB

and more importantly the Biblical doctrine of VPP and the perfection of the Hebrew, Aramaic, and Greek words behind the KJB.

[17] Charles Seet, "A Positional Paper on the Doctrine of Inspiration and Preservation of the Holy Scriptures," (http://web.singnet.com.sg/~sbseet/position.htm, accessed on February 3, 2006.)

[18] The Dean Burgon Oath states, "I swear in the name of the triune God—Father, Son and Holy Spirit—that the Bible is none other than the voice of Him that sitteth upon the throne. Every book of it, every chapter of it, every verse of it, every word of it, every syllable of it, every letter of it, is the direct utterance of the Most High. The Bible is none other than the Word of God, not some part of it more, some part of it less, but all alike the utterance of Him that sitteth upon the throne, faultless, unerring, supreme. So help me God. Amen."

[19] "Explanation of Our Non-VPP Stand," 2.

[20] See "Biblical Answers to Questions on the KJB and its Underlying Texts: A Response to Gary Hudson's 'Questions for the KJB-Only Cult,'" at www.febc.edu.sg under "Articles on the Defence of the Biblical Doctrine of Verbal Plenary Preservation of the Bible."

[21] In an earlier draft of "KJB-Only Q&A" dated July 18, 2002, I answered Hudson's question in the following way: "The question is rather mischievous. Let us rephrase it: Can a flawed Bible ever be deemed the 'Word of God?' Can a perfect God ever give His people a less than perfect Bible? The answer is obvious. The Bible is God's Word, and if God is perfect, His Word must be no less perfect. God assures us that His Word is 'very pure' (Ps 119:40), 'perfect' (Ps 19:7), 'true and righteous altogether' (Ps 19:9). All, not some or most, of Scripture is God-breathed (2 Tim 3:16)."

[22] B F Westcott and F J A Hort, *Introduction to the New Testament in the Original Greek* (New York: Harper and Brothers, , 1882); Kurt Aland and Barbara Aland, *The Text of the New Testament* (Grand Rapids: Eerdmans, 1987); Bruce Metzger, *The Text of the New Testament* (New York: Oxford University Press, 1992).

[23]   D A Carson, *The King James Version Debate* (Grand Rapids: Baker, 1979); James R White, *The King James Only Controversy* (Minneapolis: Bethany, 1995).

[24]   James B Williams, ed, *From the Mind of God to the Mind of Man* (Greenville: Ambassador-Emerald, 1999); James B Williams and Randolf Shaylor, eds, *God's Word in Our Hands* (Greenville: Ambassador-Emerald, 2003); Roy E Beacham and Kevin T Bauder, eds, *One Bible Only?* (Grand Rapids: Kregel, 2001).

[25]   Paisley, *My Plea for the Old Sword*; D A Waite, *Defending the King James Bible* (Collingswood: Bible For Today, 1996); Timothy Tow and Jeffrey Khoo, *A Theology for Every Christian: Knowing God and His Word* (Singapore, FEBC Press, 1998).

[26]   "A Doctrinal Positional Statement of Life B-P Church," states, "We do employ the KJB alone as our primary scriptural text in the public reading, preaching, and teaching of the English Bible." *50 Years Building His Kingdom*, Life Bible-Presbyterian Church Golden Jubilee Magazine, 2000, 67.

[27]   See George Skariah, "The Biblical Doctrine of the Perfect Preservation of the Holy Scriptures," ThD dissertation, Far Eastern Bible College, 2005.

[28]   Timothy Tow, "God's Special Providential Care of the Text of Scripture," *Bible Witness*, October-December 2002, 3-4.

[29]   S H Tow, "Gospel Safeguard—VPP," Calvary Pandan B-P Church Weekly, January 1, 2006. See also his book, *Beyond Versions: A Biblical Perspective of Modern English Bibles* (Singapore: King James Productions, 1998).

[30]   Ibid.

LESSON 9

Identification Of God's Preserved Words II

(Continued From Lesson 8)

Canon, Texts, and Words: Lost and Found or Preserved and Identified?

I. INTRODUCTION

The Judeo-Christian Bible comprising the Old Testament (OT) and the New Testament (NT) Scriptures is usually discussed in terms of its respective canons, texts, and words in the original languages. As seen in our previous discussion[1], there is no issue with the divine inspiration of the Scriptures in the original writings or autographs. The issue today involves the transmission of the Scriptures from the time they were originally written until the present day. Since the autographs, the original scripts written by the original writers themselves, no longer exist, having long perished, can Bible-believers today say they have in their possession the very same Scriptures or Words that God had originally given by divine inspiration?

Many modern pastors and scholars deny that there exists such an infallible and inerrant Bible today. Although they may believe in the Verbal Plenary Inspiration (VPI), they do not believe in the Verbal Plenary Preservation (VPP) of the Holy Scriptures. In their minds, the inspiration of the Scripture is a miracle from God, but the preservation of Scripture is man's work without any special superintendence or intervention by God.[2] Such a view is held nowadays by those who call themselves "Reformed." The "Reformed" pastors and teachers of today actually speak in a Bibliological tongue that is strange to the ears of the Reformed scholars and Reformation saints. This strange understanding of the Bible that is far removed from the Reformed faith concerns looking at the infallibility and inerrancy of the Bible only in terms of (1) its divine inspiration and not divine preservation, and (2) its autographs and not apographs.[3]

In view of the current fallacious paradigm and ignorant confusion over the nature of the Sacred Scriptures of yesterday and today, it is the intention of this paper to recapture the true Biblical teaching and Reformed thinking of the Scriptures, that (1) the verbally inspired Scriptures are verbally preserved by God and God alone; and (2) the supremely authoritative Scriptures are the extant infallible apographs and not the non-existent autographs. As such (1) the inspired Scriptures were never lost but always preserved without any corruption or missing words; (2) the Sacred Scriptures are *always infallible and inerrant*, and *supremely authoritative not only in the days of the Reformation, but also today—Sola Scriptura!*

This paper seeks to identify where and what the infallible and inerrant Scriptures are in terms of their Canon, Texts, and Words.

II. CANON

The word "canonicity" comes from the Greek *kanon* which means "a straight rod," or "a measuring rule." When applied to the Scriptures, it means the standard list of divinely inspired *books*—the Word of God—which serves as the only authoritative basis for the faith and practice of the Church.

A. Old Testament Canon

By the time of Jesus, the OT Canon was already completed and identified. The Jews regarded the 39 books of the *Tanakh* (the Hebrew OT Canon) comprising the (1) *Torah* (Law), the *Nabi'im* (Prophets), and the *Kethubim* (Writings) to be nothing short of the direct utterance of the Most High, absolutely infallible and supremely authoritative. These 39 books were recognised as the divinely inspired books for they came during the period of Biblical revelation—the period between Moses (1450 BC) and Malachi (450 BC).

OLD TESTAMENT CANON AND BOOKS		
Canon	Books	Period
Torah (Law)	Genesis	15th Century BC
	Exodus	
	Leviticus	
	Numbers	
	Deuteronomy	
Nabi'im (Prophets)	Joshua	15th – 14th Century BC
	Judges	14th – 11th Century BC
	1 Samuel	12th – 11th Century BC
	2 Samuel	11th – 10th Century BC
	1 Kings	10th – 9th Century BC
	2 Kings	9th – 6th Century BC
	Isaiah	8th –7th Century BC
	Jeremiah	7th – 6th Century BC
	Ezekiel	6th Century BC
	Hosea	8th Century BC
	Joel	9th Century BC
	Amos	8th Century BC
	Obadiah	9th Century BC
	Jonah	8th Century BC
	Micah	8th Century BC
	Nahum	7th Century BC
	Habakkuk	7th Century BC
	Zephaniah	7th Century BC
	Haggai	6th Century BC
	Zechariah	6th Century BC
	Malachi	5th Century BC
Kethubim (Writings)	Psalms	11th – 10th Century BC
	Job	20th – 16th Century BC
	Proverbs	10th Century BC

Ruth	13th – 12th Century BC
Song of Solomon	10th Century BC
Ecclesiastes	10th Century BC
Lamentations	6th Century BC
Esther	5th Century BC
Daniel	7th – 6th Century BC
Ezra	6th Century BC
Nehemiah	5th Century BC
1 Chronicles	11th – 10th Century BC
2 Chronicles	10th – 6th Century BC

The above identification of the OT Canon is given by the Author of the Canon Himself—the Lord Jesus Christ—in Luke 24:44, "And he said unto them, These are the words which I spake unto you, while I was yet with you, that all things must be fulfilled, which were written in the *law* of Moses, and in the *prophets*, and in the *psalms*, concerning me."

The Law of Moses, the Prophets, and the Psalms/Writings make up the 39 books of the OT Canon that Jesus regarded as the very Word of God. Note that there is no mention of the Apocrypha—the 14 books[4] written during the 400 "silent years" of the inter-testamental period when there was no prophetic voice until John the Baptiser came onto the scene. The Westminster Confession of Faith (WCF) acknowledged the traditional and ecclesiastical view that the apocryphal books were not divinely inspired but merely human books with some historical value, but no spiritual or doctrinal value whatsoever:

…"The books commonly called Apocrypha, not being of divine inspiration, are no part of the canon of the Scripture, and therefore are of no authority in the Church of God, nor to be any otherwise approved, or made use of, than other human writings" (I:III).

It is a Biblical fact that God had intended a fixed number of 39 divinely inspired OT books to serve as the supremely authoritative Standard of faith and life for the Church. If there is such a divinely ordained set of canonical books for the OT, surely a similar set of canonical books can be expected for the NT.

B. New Testament Canon

The Lord Jesus Christ in fulfilment of the *Tanakh*—the OT Canon—was born of a virgin, lived a sinlessly perfect life, died on the cross for the sins of the world, was buried, and on the third day rose from the dead just as the OT Scriptures had predicted. His life and work on earth marked the beginning of the New Covenant period of a better administration of the Covenant of Grace which called for an NT Canon to regulate the life and faith of New Covenant saints.

At Pentecost, God did not present the Bible to the New Covenant Church as a complete whole. The NT Canon like the OT Canon required a period of time for its inscripturation and completion. This period of divinely inspired inscripturation occurred during the time of the Apostles of Jesus Christ. It began with the Gospel of Matthew in AD 40 and ended with the Revelation of John in AD 90.

Since Jesus gave no explicit word concerning the number of NT books and their specific identities, how did the Church finally arrive at the 27 books? It is a question that needs to be answered especially today when the Church is being attacked by pop-modernism that questions the authenticity and certainty of the 27 books that form our NT Canon. Dan Brown's bestseller—*The Da Vinci Code*—for instance speaks of the newly discovered Gnostic Gospels of Nag Hammadi as the authentic and authoritative NT books. Brown dismissed the Four Gospels of Matthew, Mark, Luke and John in the NT Canon today as fabricated accounts of the life of Christ produced in the time of Emperor Constantine (4th century AD). According to him, these Four Gospels should be rejected and replaced by the Gnostic Gospels.[5] In other words, the true Gospels were once lost but are now found!

This begs the question of whether the Church has been reading from the wrong Gospels all these centuries. Were the true books about the life of Christ lost very early and now found? Or were the true books the ones that God has preserved from the beginning, and received by the Church from the time they were written until today? By virtue of God's promise of the preservation of His words in Psalm 12:6-7, Matthew 5:18, 24:35, John 10:35, and 1 Peter 1:23-25, we believe the latter to be true—that the all-powerful Author of the Christian Scriptures has supernaturally and continuously preserved His words throughout the ages, and kept them pure and uncorrupted, available and accessible to His Church, so that His people might appeal to them as their supremely authoritative Canon or rule of faith and practice without any doubt or uncertainty.

Nevertheless, Brown's pop-modernistic attack on the Scriptures does great damage to the testimony of the Scriptures and of the Church. Ben Witherington III highlighted the serious implications of Brown's canonical-critical book:

> "The issue of canon—what books constitute the final authority for Christians—is no small matter. If the critics are correct, then Christianity must indeed be radically reinterpreted, just as they suggest. If they are wrong, traditional Christians have their work cut out for them, because many seekers remain skeptical of claims to biblical authority." [6]

To put it bluntly: No Canon, no Christ; no Canon, no Gospel!

Was the Biblical Canon falsified and the Christian Gospel fabricated? There was in fact no "orthodox" fabrication of the Gospels as posited by Brown but the very opposite. History reveals the unorthodox corruption of the Scriptures by Alexandrian heretics who denied and attacked the full deity of Christ.[7] It is a fact that shortly after the inspired NT books were completed, spurious books claiming inspiration were also written (eg, Acts of Paul, Revelation of Peter, Epistle of Barnabas, Gospel of Peter, Gospel of Thomas, Acts of Andrew etc).[8] The contents of these false books do not fit the nature of divinely inspired writ. They are filled with myths and even blasphemous stories of Christ. The born again and Spirit indwelt believer can tell straightaway that these books are not of God (John 16:13, 1 Cor 2:12-14, 1 John 2:27). The early believers had long rejected them as spurious.

So how was the NT Canon arrived at? The Canon was arrived at by the ecclesiastical consensus of God's people who were indwelt and led by the Holy Spirit (John 16:13). The Council of Carthage (397), chaired by the pre-eminent early church father and theologian—Augustine—identified the sacred books by name. There were exactly 27 of them.

NEW TESTAMENT CANON AND BOOKS		
Canon	Books	Date
Gospels	Matthew	AD 40
	Mark	AD 45
	Luke	AD 45-55
	John	AD 70-90
History	Acts	AD 62-64
Epistles	Romans	AD 55
	1 Corinthians	AD 54
	2 Corinthians	AD 55
	Galatians	AD 49
	Ephesians	AD 60
	Philippians	AD 60
	Colossians	AD 60
	1 Thessalonians	AD 50-51
	2 Thessalonians	AD 50-51
	1 Timothy	AD 62
	2 Timothy	AD 63
	Titus	AD 62
	Philemon	AD 60
	Hebrews	AD 60-65
	James	AD 40-44
	1 Peter	AD 63
	2 Peter	AD 63-64
	1 John	AD 80-90
	2 John	AD 80-90
	3 John	AD 80-90
	Jude	AD 60-70
Apocalypse	Revelation	AD 90

The Canon of NT books above was no innovation, but an official statement of what the Church by ecclesiastical consensus had already accepted as inspired Scripture by virtue of its divine origination. The WCF states:

We may be moved and induced by the testimony of the Church to an high and reverent esteem of the Holy Scripture. And the heavenliness of the matter, the efficacy of the doctrine, the majesty of the style, the consent of all the parts, the scope of the whole (which is, to give all glory to God), the full discovery it makes of the only way of man's salvation, the many other incomparable excellencies, and the entire perfection thereof, are arguments whereby it doth abundantly evidence itself to be the Word of God: yet notwithstanding, our full persuasion and assurance of the infallible truth and divine authority thereof, is from the inward work of the Holy Spirit bearing witness by and with the Word in our hearts (I:V).

The NT Canon is under attack today like never before. Bible-believing Christians ought not to be naïve but to put on the whole armour of God (Eph 6:11-18). We ought to realize that truth is ascertained by spiritual knowledge, and we need to pray for the Holy Spirit to guide us into all truth (John 16:13).

III. TEXTS

The texts of the Holy Scriptures refer to the copies of the Scriptures which come either in handwritten or in printed form.

A. Old Testament Text

The OT Scriptures were first given to Israel—God's chosen nation. Romans 3:1-2 tells us that God had committed to the Jews the safekeeping and copying of the Holy Scriptures. Knowing well the divine nature of the Scriptures, that the words of the sacred pages were the very words of the Almighty God, they copied the Scriptures with great precision and accuracy employing the following rules:

1. The parchment must be made from the skin of clean animals; must be prepared by a Jew only, and the skins must be fastened together by strings taken from clean animals.

2. Each column must be no less than 48 and no more than 60 lines. The entire copy must be first lined, and if three words were written in it without the line, the copy was worthless.

3. The ink must be of no other color than black, and it must be prepared according to a special recipe.

4. No word or letter could be written from memory; the scribe must have an authentic copy before him, and he must read and pronounce aloud each word before writing it.

5. He must reverently wipe his pen each time before writing the word for "God," and must wash his whole body before writing the word "Jehovah," lest the holy name be contaminated.

6. Strict rules were given concerning the forms of the letters, spaces between letters, words, and sections, the use of the pen, the color of the parchment, etc.

7. The revision of a roll must be made within 30 days after the work was finished; otherwise it was worthless. One mistake on a sheet condemned the sheet; if three mistakes were found on any page, the entire manuscript was condemned.

8. Every word and every letter was counted, and if a letter were omitted, an extra letter inserted, or if one letter touched another, the manuscript was condemned and destroyed at once. [9]

These very strict rules of transcription show how precious the Jews had regarded the inspired words of God, and how precise their copying of these inspired words must have been. Such strict practices in copying "give us strong encouragement to believe that we have the real Old Testament, *the same one* which our Lord had and which was originally given by inspiration of God." [10]

The present confusion in identifying the Hebrew Scriptures is not with the traditional copies which God has kept pure without corruption by His special providence, but with the printed editions of the Hebrew Text which comes in two types: (1) the Hebrew Masoretic Text—Ben Chayyim (1524-25), and (2) the Biblia Hebraica—Kittel (1937) and Stuttgart (1967/77).

The Ben Chayyim Text is the faithful text that follows the traditional and providentially preserved manuscripts. This Hebrew Text underlying the KJB is totally infallible and inerrant. The Ben Chayyim Text is published today by the Trinitarian Bible Society (TBS). TBS considers the Ben Chayyim Masoretic Text to be the definitive Hebrew Text for today. [11]

The Kittel and Stuttgart texts, on the other hand, display a critical apparatus that is filled with conjectural emendations that come from modern scholarship. These modern critical texts are the texts that underlie the NASV, NIV, and NKJB. The Kittel and Stuttgart texts contain 20,000-30,000 suggested corrections or changes to the OT Scriptures.[12] Many of these recommended corrections are unwarranted because they come from the Dead Sea Scrolls (DSS), or the Samaritan Pentateuch which trace their origins to heretical sects (eg, Essenes and Samaritans, cf John 4:22), and dubious translations like the Septuagint (LXX).[13] The textual-critical apparatuses found in these critical texts cause the Bible student to doubt God's Word. They cause him to question whether he has indeed all the words of Scripture and whether the words of Scripture can be trusted as being altogether true—the very words of God—verbally inspired and preserved (Matt 5:18)? From personal experience, having practised the textual-critical methods of modern scholarship at both Bible College and Seminary levels, I can testify that such critical devices in the modern texts not only cast doubt on God's Word, but also distract from a reverent and faithful study to a prideful and judgmental study of the Holy Scriptures.

In light of the Biblical doctrine of the divine, verbal and plenary preservation of the Scriptures, Bible-believing students would do well to stick to the providentially preserved line of traditional Hebrew manuscripts and text which is the Ben Chayyim Masoretic Text—the Text that underlies the time-tested and time-honoured KJB—over against the new and critical line of modernistic texts that are behind all the modern English versions.

B. New Testament Text

The NT Scriptures were written by the Apostles of Jesus Christ under divine inspiration (2 Tim 3:16). The NT Scriptures were then committed to the care of the NT Church comprising born again believers who are loyal to both the Living Word and the Written Word. Just like the OT Scripture, the Lord has also promised to preserve the inspired Greek words of the NT Scripture. Three times Jesus said, "Heaven and earth shall pass away, but my words shall not pass away" (Matt 24:35, Mark 13:31, Luke 21:33).

The NT autographs in time became apographs for they were copied and circulated to all the NT churches for their meditation, application and edification. As the Church grew, the copies multiplied. There are over 5000 extant NT copies today. These 5000 plus manuscripts are classified under two categories: Byzantine and Alexandrian. [14]

	TWO STREAMS OF TEXTS AND VERSIONS	
	Preserved Byzantine/Majority/Received Text	Perverted Alexandrian/Minority/WH Text
Text	Every word preserved	Many words excised
Thrust	Spirit of the 16th Century Reformation	Spirit of 19th and 20th Century Modernism
Translators	Martyrs and Reformers—Wycliffe, Tyndale, Coverdale, and KJB men	Money-Makers, Liberals, Ecumenists, and Neo-Evangelicals
Technique	Verbal Equivalence—word for word translation	Dynamic Equivalence—thought for thought interpretation
Translation	Protestant Reformation Bible—the AV/KJB is the best. Vital doctrines fully preserved	Ecumenical and Modern Versions. Vital doctrines (virgin birth, deity of Christ, blood of Christ, Trinity, ecclesiastical separation) attacked

The Byzantine manuscripts come from the region of Byzantium or Constantinople, the capital of the Eastern or Greek Empire (AD 295-1453). The majority of the 5000 plus extant NT copies are Byzantine manuscripts. These manuscripts were faithfully copied and continuously used by the Church. They reflect uniform readings. Although there were minor variations, these were easily rectified by a simple comparison of the manuscripts.[15] The Lord has certainly kept these manuscripts pure and uncorrupted throughout the centuries. The Church recognized them to be the inspired and preserved manuscripts, and received them as the Holy Scriptures. These handwritten copies were finally put into print in the 15th century upon the invention of the printing press. During the Protestant Reformation the Lord specially raised up Erasmus, Stephanus, and Beza to prepare the Byzantine manuscripts for print. The printed Greek text eventually became known as the Textus Receptus—the Text received by all. This is the Greek text that underlies the KJB and all the other Reformation translations.[16]

The Alexandrian manuscripts come from Alexandria, Egypt. These manuscripts are in the minority, and they reveal a corrupt hand.[17] The most notorious of these minority manuscripts are the Codex Sinaiticus and the Codex Vaticanus. The Codex Sinaiticus was discovered by Tischendorf in St Catherine's monastery in Egypt in 1844 while the Codex Vaticanus was kept in the Vatican library and found in 1481. Both these manuscripts were dated to about 350 AD. Since they were such old manuscripts, and regarded by Westcott and Hort to be closest to the autographs, they were hailed as the best manuscripts in existence. Westcott and Hort then proceeded to revise the Textus Receptus based on their textual-critical theory that the older, harder, and shorter readings of the Alexandrian manuscripts were better. In 1881, they published their new but mutilated text which changed the traditional Received Text in nearly 10,000 places.[18]

God did not allow such an attack on His preserved words to go unchallenged. He raised up a most worthy scholar in Dean Burgon to expose the corruptions of the Alexandrian manuscripts on which Westcott and Hort built their revised Greek Text. Burgon, by a diligent study of the primary sources and a careful investigation of the facts, rightly judged the Alexandrian manuscripts to be among

> the most scandalously corrupt copies extant: exhibit the most shamefully mutilated texts which are anywhere to be met with: have become, by whatever process (for their history is wholly unknown), the depositories of the largest amount of fabricated readings, ancient blunders, and intentional perversions of Truth, which are discoverable in any known copies of the Word of God.[19]

Since 1881, the corrupt Westcott-Hort text has unfortunately become the standard text for modern translations of the Bible.[20] Are the Alexandrian manuscripts so reliable? The Alexandrian manuscripts and the Westcott-Hort text that underlie the modern versions of the English Bible are today being questioned by their very editors—Kurt

Aland and Barbara Aland—who wrote, "In the twentieth century the papyri have eroded the dominance of the uncials, and a group of minuscules presently under study promises to diminish it further."[21] One such papyrus is the Magdalen GR17 or "Jesus Papyrus" which consists of three fragments containing Matthew 26:7-8, 26:10, 14, 15, 22, 23, 31, 32, 33. It is a very early, first century (AD 60) manuscript. The last four words of Matthew 26:22 (*legein auto hekastos auton*) in the GR17 agree with the Textus Receptus over against the Westcott-Hort and modern critical texts (*legein auto heis hekastos*).[22] Another evidence of the antiquity and authenticity of the Textus Receptus comes from the Chester Beatty Papyri which are early 3rd century fragments and they agree with the Traditional or Byzantine Text. Papyrus p75 contains the ascension of Christ (Luke 24:51) which was omitted in the Westcott-Hort Text and modern versions like the NASV.[23] Now, the 26th edition of the critical text of Nestle and Aland has put the ascension verse back into the original text bringing it to conformity with the inspired and preserved Textus Receptus underlying the KJB.[24] All such findings confirm Dean Burgon's observation all along—the Alexandrian/Minority/Westcott-Hort texts are the heretically corrupted texts, but the Byzantine/Majority/Received texts are the divinely preserved texts.[25]

It is tragic that in many Bible Colleges and Seminaries today, the genealogy of the NT apographs follows the textual-critical paradigm invented by Westcott and Hort who had introduced an imaginative transmission history of the NT Text that is vastly different from the Biblical truth of VPP that is taught by the Author of the Scriptures Himself in His forever infallible and inerrant Word (Ps 12:6-7, Matt 5:18, 24:35, John 10:35, 1 Pet 1:23-25). Far Eastern Bible College (FEBC), despite fierce local and foreign opposition to her VPP belief, remains steadfast in its defence of God's forever infallible and inerrant Word. The 100% inspired Word of God are in the 100% preserved words of the Hebrew Masoretic Text (Ben Chayyim), and the Greek Textus Receptus (Stephanus, Beza, Scrivener) underlying the time-tested and time-honoured King James or Authorized Version.[26]

IV. WORDS

The words of the Scriptures are important (Deut 8:3, Matt 4:4, Luke 4:4). God uses His words to communicate His Truth so that we might know who and what He is and how we might be saved through Him. The Bible clearly tells us that it is God's written words (pasa graphe—"All Scripture") that are inspired (2 Tim 3:16), and from these inspired words come all the doctrines that are sufficient and profitable for the spiritual growth and maturity of the believer (2 Tim 3:17). The Bible also clearly says that God Himself will preserve all His inspired words to the jot and tittle without the loss of any word, letter or syllable (Ps 12:6-7, Matt 5:18, 24:35).

A. Old Testament Words

Now if we have the inspired, infallible and inerrant words of God today preserved in the traditional and Reformation Scriptures, then how do we explain the differences or discrepancies found in the Bible especially those found in 1 Samuel 13:1, 2 Chronicles 22:2, and many other places. Can these be due to "scribal errors"?

Since God has preserved His inspired words to the last iota and no words are lost but all kept pure and intact in the original language Scriptures, we must categorically deny that our Bible contains any mistake or error (scribal or otherwise). But it is sad that certain evangelicals and fundamentalists would rather choose to deny the present infallibility and inerrancy of the Holy Scriptures by considering the "discrepancies" found in 1 Samuel 13:1 and 2 Chronicles 22:2 and other like passages to be *actual* instead of *apparent* discrepancies, and calling them "scribal errors."

A denial of the verbal preservation of the Scriptures will invariably lead one to believe that some words of God have been lost and remain lost leading to a "scribal error" view of the OT Scriptures. For instance, W Edward Glenny denies that God has perfectly preserved His Word so that no words have been lost. He says, "The evidence from the OT text suggests that such is not the case. *We might have lost a few words* ...″[27] Based on his "lost words" view of the Bible, he was quick to point out "obvious discrepancies" in the OT like 2 Chronicles 22:2. He pontificates,

In 1 Chronicles 8:26 [sic], the KJB states that Ahaziah was twenty-two when he began to reign; the parallel in 2 Chronicles 22:2 says that he began to reign at the age of forty-two. ... These *obvious discrepancies* in the KJB and the Hebrew manuscripts on which it is based show that *none of them perfectly preserved the inspired autographa.*[28]

Now, know that 2 Chronicles 22:2 reads "forty-two" in the KJB and RSV. A number of the modern versions like the NASV, NIV, and ESV read "twenty-two" instead. So which is the original, inspired reading: "forty-two" (in KJB, and RSV), or "twenty-two" (in NASV, NIV, and ESV)? In making such a textual decision, we must have a perfect standard, and that infallible and inerrant standard is the inspired and preserved Hebrew Scripture, and not any translation ancient or modern.

It is significant to note that every single Hebrew manuscript reads "forty-two" (*arebba'im wushetha'im*) in 2 Chronicles 22:2. There is no evidence of lost words—every word to the letter is preserved, and reads precisely as "forty-two" as accurately translated in the KJB and RSV. If every Hebrew manuscript reads "forty-two" in 2 Chronicles 22:2, then on what basis do the NASV, NIV, and ESV change it to "twenty-two"? They change "forty-two" to "twenty-two" on the basis of the Septuagint (LXX) which is a Greek version of the Hebrew Scripture just like the NIV is an English version of it. In other words, they use a version or translation to correct the original Hebrew text! Should not it be the other way round?

Why do they do this? They do this because of their fallacious assumption that (1) God did not preserve His words perfectly, (2) lost words exist in the Hebrew text, and (3) 2 Chronicles 22:2 is an "obvious" discrepancy (cf 2 Kgs 8:26). Thus, Glenny and all such non-VPPists are quick to use a fallible translation (eg, LXX) to correct the infallible Hebrew Text! This is no different from someone using the NIV today to correct any part of the Hebrew Text according to his whim and fancy! But Glenny calls it "conjectural emendation" which sounds scholarly but colloquially it means—"*Suka* only, change!" Can a translation be more inspired than or superior to the original language text? Can a translation or version (whatever the language) be used to correct the Hebrew? Glenny's method of explaining such "obvious discrepancies" in the Bible is troubling for it displays (1) a sceptical attitude towards the numerical integrity of God's Word, (2) a critical readiness to deny the present inerrancy of Scripture in historical details, and (3) a lackadaisical approach towards solving difficulties in the Bible by conveniently dismissing such difficulties as "scribal errors."

A godly approach is one that presupposes the present infallibility and inerrancy of God's Word not only when it speaks on salvation, but also when it speaks on history, geography or science. "*Let God be true, but every man a liar*" (Rom 3:4). Such a godly approach to difficult passages is seen in Robert J Sargent who, by comparing (not correcting) Scripture with Scripture, offered two possible solutions to the so-called "problem" or "error" in 2 Chronicles 22:2. Sargent suggested that "forty-two" could be either (1) Ahaziah's years counted from the beginning of the dynasty founded by Omri, or (2) the year in which Ahaziah was actually seated as king though anointed as one at "twenty-two" (2 Kgs 8:26).[29] Whatever the answer may be, the truth and fact is: the inspired and preserved Hebrew reading in 2 Chronicles 22:2 is "forty-two" and not "twenty-two," and no man has the right to change or correct God's Word by "conjectural emendation," taking heed to the serious warning not to add to or subtract from the Holy Scriptures (Rev 22:18-19).

Now, let us look at the next text which is 1 Samuel 13:1 which the KJB translates as, "Saul reigned one year." But the other versions read quite differently. The NASV has, "Saul was *forty* years old when he began to reign;" the NIV has, "Saul was *thirty* years old when he became king;" and the RSV has, "Saul was ... years old when he began to reign." Which of the above is correct? The only way whereby we can ascertain the correct reading is to go to the Hebrew Bible. The Hebrew Bible since day one reads *Ben-shanah Shaoul*, literally, "A son of a year (was) Saul," or idiomatically, "Saul was a year old."

Now, the difficulty is: How could Saul be only a year old when he began to reign? Scholars and translators who do not believe in the perfect preservation of the Scriptures say that this is an actual discrepancy in the Hebrew Text which they attribute to a "scribal error." This is why Michael Harding in a mistitled book—*God's Word in Our Hands*—wrote,

[I]n 1 Samuel 13:1-2 the Masoretic Text states that Saul was one year of age (*ben-shanah*—literally "son of a year") ... Some ancient Greek manuscripts ... read "thirty years" instead of "one year," ... On account of my theological conviction regarding the inerrancy of the autographa, I believe the original Hebrew text also reads "thirty," even though *we do not currently possess a Hebrew manuscript with that reading.*[30]

Harding and those like him fail to apply the logic of faith to the promise of God that He will preserve and has preserved every iota of His inspired words. This leads them to conclude that a word is lost and 2 Chronicles 22:2 contains a "scribal error" even when there is no such error to begin with. They change the text when the text needs no changing. They replace divine words with human words. Instead of attributing error to the translation (LXX, NASV, NIV, RSV), they rather fault the inspired and preserved Hebrew Text and treat it as an actual discrepancy even when there is absolutely none. This has caused many Bible believers to doubt God's Word: Do we really have God's infallible and inerrant Word in our hands? Many are indeed stumbled by such allegations of error in the Bible, and are questioning whether they can really trust the Scriptures at all if there is no such thing as a complete and perfect Word of God today.

It must be categorically stated that there is no error at all in the Hebrew Text and no mistake also in the KJB which translated 1 Samuel 13:1 accurately. So how do we explain 1 Samuel 13:1? A faithful explanation is offered by Matthew Poole who wrote,

[Saul] had now reigned one year, from his first election at Mizpeh, in which time these things were done, which are recorded in chap. xi., xii., to wit, peaceably, or righteously. Compare 2 Sam. ii.10. [31]

In other words, the year of Saul was calculated not from the time of his birth but from his *appointment as king*; "Saul was a year old *into his reign*." This meaning is supported by the Geneva Bible which reads, "*Saul now had beene King one yeere.*" Rest assured, there is no mistake in the Hebrew Text and in the KJB here. God has indeed inspired and preserved His OT words perfectly so that we might have an infallible, inerrant OT Bible in our hands today.

B. New Testament Words

As much as the Lord has preserved His inspired OT words (Matt 5:18), so also has He preserved His inspired NT words (Matt 24:35). Where are His words? The divinely preserved words of God today are found in the pure and preserved Greek Textus Receptus underlying the KJB, and not in the corrupt and heretical Westcott-Hort Greek Text behind the modern versions which not only cast doubts on the authenticity of certain Biblical passages like the last 12 verses of Mark (Mark 16:9-20), and the *pericope de adultera* (John 7:53-8:11), but also scissored out the following verses of Scripture in whole or in part:

SCISSION AND CORRUPTION IN THE WESTCOTT-HORT TEXT AND THE MODERN ENGLISH VERSIONS

Entire Verses Deleted

Matt	17:21	Howbeit this kind goeth not out but by prayer and fasting.
	18:11	For the Son of man is come to save that which was lost.
	23:14	Woe unto you, scribes and Pharisees, hypocrites! for ye devour widows' houses, and for a pretence make long prayer: therefore ye shall receive the greater damnation.
Mark	7:16	If any man have ears to hear, let him hear.
	9:44	Where their worm dieth not, and the fire is not quenched.
	9:46	Where their worm dieth not, and the fire is not quenched.
	11:26	But if ye do not forgive, neither will your Father which is in heaven forgive your trespasses.
	15:28	And the scripture was fulfilled, which saith, And he was numbered with the transgressors.
Luke	17:36	Two *men* shall be in the field; the one shall be taken, and the other left.
	23:17	(For of necessity he must release one unto them at the feast.)
John	5:4	For an angel went down at a certain season into the pool, and troubled the water: whosoever then first after the troubling of the water stepped in was made whole of whatsoever disease he had.
Acts	8:37	And Philip said, If thou believest with all thine heart, thou mayest. And he answered and said, I believe that Jesus Christ is the Son of God.
	15:34	Notwithstanding it pleased Silas to abide there still.
	24:7	But the chief captain Lysias came *upon us*, and with great violence took *him* away out of our hands.
	28:29	And when he had said these words, the Jews departed, and had great reasoning among themselves.
Rom	16:24	The grace of our Lord Jesus Christ *be* with you all. Amen.

Portions of Verses Deleted or Changed

Matt	5:22	without a cause
	5:27	by them of old time
	6:13	For thine is the kingdom and the power and the glory forever. Amen

	9:35	among the people
	10:3	Lebbaeus, whose surname was
	10:8	raise the dead
	12:35,	of the heart
	13:51	Jesus saith unto them
	15:8	draweth nigh unto me with their mouth
	18:29	at his feet
	19:20	from my youth
	20:7	and whatsoever is right, that shall ye receive
	20:16	For many be called, but few chosen
	20:22	and to be baptized with the baptism that I am baptized with
	20:23	and to be baptized with the baptism that I am baptized with
	22:13	take him away, and
	23:3	observe
	25:13	wherein the Son of Man cometh
	26:60	false witnesses
	27:35	that it might be fulfilled which was spoken by the prophet: They parted my garments among them, and upon my vesture did they cast lots
Mark	1:2	Isaiah the prophet
	1:14	of the kingdom
	2:17	to repentance
	3:5	whole as the other
	3:15	to heal sicknesses and
	4:4	of the air
	6:11	Verily, I say unto you, It shall be more tolerable for Sodom and Gomorrha in the day of judgment than for that city
	6:36	bread, for they have nothing to eat
	7:2	they found fault
	9:29	and fasting
	9:45	into the fire that never shall be quenched
	9:49	and every sacrifice shall be salted with salt
	10:24	for them that trust in riches
	11:10	in the name of the Lord
	12:4	and at him they cast stones
	12:30	This is the first commandment
	12:33	with all the soul
	13:14	spoken of by Daniel the prophet

	14:19	And another said, Is it I?
	14:27	because of me this night
	14:70	and thy speech agreeth thereto
Luke	1:28	blessed art thou among women
	1:29	when she saw him
	1:78	hath visited
	4:4	but by every word of God
	4:8	Get thee behind me, Satan
	4:18	to heal the brokenhearted
	4:41	Christ
	5:38	and both are preserved
	6:10	whole as the other
	6:45	treasure of his heart
	7:10	that had been sick
	7:31	And the Lord said
	8:45	and they that were with him
	8:45	and sayest thou, Who touched me?
	8:54	and he put them all out
	9:54	even as Elias did
	9:55	and said, Ye know not what manner of spirit ye are of
	9:56	For the Son of man is not come to destroy men's lives, but to save them
	10:35	when he departed
	11:2	Thy will be done, as in heaven, so in earth
	11:4	but deliver us from evil
	11:11	bread of any of you that is a father, will he give him a stone? or if he ask
	11:29	the prophet
	11:44	scribes and Pharisees, hypocrites
	11:54	that they might accuse him
	17:3	against thee
	17:9	him? I trow not
	19:5	and saw him
	20:23	Why tempt ye me?
	20:30	took her to wife, and he died childless
	22:30	in my kingdom
	22:31	And the Lord said
	22:64	struck him on the face and
	22:68	me, nor let me go
	23:23	and of the chief priests
	23:38	written over him in letters of Greek, and Latin, and Hebrew
	24:1	and certain others with them
	24:42	and of an honeycomb

John	3:13	which is in heaven
	3:15	not perish, but
	4:42	the Christ
	5:3	waiting for the moving of the water
	5:16	and sought to slay him
	6:11	to the disciples, and the disciples
	6:22	whereinto his disciples were entered
	6:47	on me
	8:9	being convicted by their own conscience
	8:10	and saw none but the woman
	8:59	through the midst of them, and so passed by
	9:11	the pool of
	10:26	as I said unto you
	11:41	from the place where the dead was laid
	12:1	which had been dead
	17:12	in the world
	19:16	and led him away
Acts	2:23	ye have taken
	7:30	of the Lord
	7:37	him shall ye hear
	9:5	it is hard for thee to kick against the pricks
	10:6	he shall tell thee what thou oughtest to do
	10:21	which were sent unto him from Cornelius
	10:32	who, when he cometh, shall speak unto thee
	15:24	Ye must be circumcised, and keep the law
	17:5	which believed not
	18:21	I must by all means keep this feast that cometh in Jerusalem
	21:8	that were of Paul's company
	21:25	that they observe no such thing, save only
	22:9	and were afraid
	22:20	unto his death
	24:6	and would have judged according to our law
	24:8	commanding his accusers to come unto thee
	24:15	of the dead
	24:26	that he might loose him
Rom.	1:16	of Christ
	3:22	and upon all
	8:1	who walk not after the flesh, but after the Spirit
	8:26	for us
	9:31	of righteousness
	9:32	of the law
	10:15	preach the gospel of peace

	11:6	But if it be of works, then is it no more grace: otherwise work is no more work
	14:6	and he that regardeth not the day, to the Lord he doth not regard it. He that eateth, eateth to the Lord, for he giveth God thanks; and he that eateth not, to the Lord he eateth not, and giveth God thanks
	14:21	or is offended, or is made weak
	15:24	I will come to you
	15:29	of the gospel
1 Cor.	5:7	for us
	6:20	and in your spirit, which are God's
	9:18	of Christ
	10:23	for me
	10:28	for the earth is the Lord's, and the fulness thereof
	11:24	Take, eat
	11:29	Unworthily
	15:47	the Lord
2 Cor.	8:4	that we would receive
	12:11	in glorying
	13:2	I write
Gal.	3:1	that ye should not obey the truth
	3:17	in Christ
	4:7	through Christ
Eph.	3:9	by Jesus Christ
	3:14	of our Lord Jesus Christ
	4:17	other
	5:30.	of his flesh, and of his bones
Phil.	3:16	rule, let us mind the same things
Col.	1:2	and the Lord Jesus Christ
	1:14	through his blood
	2:2	and of the Father and
	2:11	of the sins
1 Thes.	1:1	from God our Father and the Lord Jesus Christ
2 Thes.	2:4	as God
1 Tim.	2:7	in Christ
	3:3	not greedy of filthy lucre
	3:16	"who" instead of "God"
	4:12	in spirit
	5:4	good and
	5:16	man or
	6:5	from such withdraw thyself
	6:7	and it is certain
2 Tim.	1:11	of the Gentiles
Heb.	1:3	by himself
	2:7	and didst set him over the works of thy hands
	3:6	firm unto the end

	8:12	and their sins
	10:9	O God
	10:30	saith the Lord
	11:11	was delivered of a child
	11:13	were persuaded of them
	12:20	or thrust through with a dart
Jas.	4:4	adulterers and
1 Pet.	1:22	through the Spirit
	4:1	for us
	4:14	on their part he is evil spoken of, but on your part he is glorified
1 John.	2:7	from the beginning
	4:3	Christ is come in the flesh
	5:7	in heaven: the Father, the Word, and the Holy Spirit; and these three are one
	5:13	and that ye may believe on the name of the Son of God
Rev.	1:8	the beginning and the ending
	1:11	I am Alpha and Omega, the first and the last: and
	1:11	which are in Asia
	5:14	him that liveth for ever and ever
	11:1	and the angel stood
	11:17	and art to come
	14:12	here are they
	15:2	over his mark
	16:5	O Lord
	16:7	another out of
	16:14	of the earth and
	19:1	the Lord
	21:24	of them which are saved

All the above words are the words God has purely preserved and kept intact in the Greek Textus Receptus on which the KJB is based, but are doubted and deleted in the modern English versions which reflect the corruptions of the Westcott-Hort Text. A total of 2886 words (equivalent to 1-2 Peter) have been scissored out of the KJB by the modern versions.[32] Which Bible is true—the "cut up" Bible that is edited by modernists and neo-evangelicals, and based on heretical and corrupt manuscripts, or the "kept pure" Bible that is sourced in the Protestant Reformation and based on divinely preserved and uncorrupted manuscripts? If the Holy Spirit indwells you and grants you discernment, the choice is obvious.

V. CONCLUSION

The conclusion of this paper is as follows:

1. The Judeo-Christian Canon was never lost and found, but always preserved and identified, and they are the 66 books of the Bible—39 in the OT, and 27 in the NT, no more and no less, fixed and firm, the Apocrypha and Gnostic Gospels having no part whatsoever.

2. The OT and NT Texts were never lost and found, but always preserved and identified, and they are the Hebrew Masoretic Text of the OT, and the Greek Textus Receptus of the NT, and not the critical and corrupt texts of Kittel/Stuttgart, and Westcott-Hort.

3. The perfectly inspired words of the Hebrew/Aramaic OT and Greek NT were never lost and found, but always preserved and identified, and they are all the words of the Hebrew Masoretic Text (Ben Chayyim) and the Greek Textus Receptus (Stephanus, Beza, Scrivener) on which the KJB—the Reformation Bible—is based, and not the interpretive or speculative words of any version ancient or modern.

In these end-times, may God's Church—"the pillar and ground of the truth"—return to the Reformed Bibliology of 16th Century Protestantism, and reject the Deformed Babelology of 20th Century Postmodernism, Neo-Evangelicalism, and Neo-Fundamentalism.
The Written Foundation of our Judeo-Christian Faith is sure and secure for "the Word of our God shall stand forever" (Isa 40:8). Amen!

NOTES

[1] Jeffrey Khoo, "Inspiration, Preservation, and Translations," a paper presented to the Truth Bible-Presbyterian Church Adults' Sunday School, March 5, 2006.

[2] For instance, Princeton Seminary's Bruce Metzger, in his textbook on New Testament textual criticism entitled, *The Text of the New Testament* (New York: Oxford University Press, 1992), discusses the New Testament text in terms of "Its Transmission, Corruption and Restoration," presuming that there is no such thing as a divinely preserved text that is without corruption, and that the restoration of the text is entirely in the hands of textual scholars and their universities, and not at all in God and His Church.

3 Jeffrey Khoo, "Sola Autographa or Sola Apographa?" *The Burning Bush* 11 (2005): 3-19. See also Theodore P Letis, *The Ecclesiastical Text* (Philadelphia: Institute for Renaissance and Reformation Biblical Studies, 1997).

[4] The word "apocrypha" comes from the Greek *kryptein* ("to hide") and speaks of the spurious nature of these 14 books: (1) 1 Esdras, (2) 2 Esdras, (3) Tobit, (4) Judith, (5) Rest of the Chapters of Esther, (6) Wisdom of Solomon, (7) Ecclesiasticus, (8) Baruch, (9) Song of the Three Holy Children, (10) History of Susanna, (11) Bel and the Dragon, (12) Prayer of Manasseh, (13) 1 Maccabees, (14) 2 Maccabees.

[5] Dan Brown, *The Da Vinci Code* (New York: Doubleday, 2003), 254. See "The Gnostic Society Library" (www.gnosis.org/library.html).

[6] Ben Witherington III, "Why the 'Lost Gospels' Lost Out," *Christianity Today* (June 2004): 28-32.

[7] See J W Burgon, *The Causes of Corruption of the Traditional Text of the Holy Gospels* (Collingswood: Dean Burgon Society, 1998 reprint). On page 13, Burgon wrote, "certain manuscripts ... particularly copies of a Version ... these do, to the present hour, bear traces incontestably of ancient mischief."

[8] See *Lost Books of the Bible Being All the Gospels, Epistles, and Other Pieces Now Extant Attributed in the First Four Centuries to*

Jesus Christ, His Apostles and Their Companions Not Included, by its Compilers, in the Authorized New Testament; and, the Recently Discovered Syriac Mss. of Pilate's Letters to Tiberius, etc. (np: Alpha House, 1926).

[9] H S Miller, *General Biblical Introduction* (Houghton: Word Bearer, 1947), 184-5.

[10] Ibid, 185.

[11] Trinitarian Bible Society, "Statement of Doctrine of Holy Scripture," *Quarterly Record* (April-June2005): 1-15.

[12] See D A Waite, *Defending the King James Bible: A Fourfold Superiority*, 2nd ed (Collingswood: Bible For Today, 1996), 20-3.

[13] J Daniel Hays in his paper, "Reconsidering the Height of Goliath," *Journal of the Evangelical Theological Society* 48 (2005): 701-14, questioned the height of Goliath (1 Sam 17:4) in the traditional and received Masoretic Text, calling "six cubits and a span" (ie, 9 feet, 9 inches) a "scribal error." He argued in favour of "four cubits and a span" (ie, 6 feet, 9 inches) as found in the DSS (4QSam), LXX, and Codex Vaticanus. Thus Goliath was not that extraordinarily tall after all, and the Jews and the Christians have been reading the wrong height of Goliath all these centuries and millennia. Such a criticism of the Bible is typical of scholars who are either ignorant or dismissive of the Biblical doctrine of VPP.

[14] Adapted from S H Tow, *Beyond Versions* (Singapore: King James Productions, 1998), 121.

[15] For a defense of the Byzantine Text, see Jakob Van Bruggen, *The Ancient Text of the New Testament* (Winnipeg: Premier, 1976); and Harry Sturz, *The Byzantine Text-Type and New Testament Textual Criticism* (Nashville: Thomas Nelson, 1984). Dr Van Bruggen is Professor of NT at the Theological College of the Reformed Churches in The Netherlands (Broederweg, Kampen), and Dr Sturz was Professor of Greek at BIOLA (Bible Institute of Los Angeles). His book was his ThD dissertation at Grace Theological Seminary, Winona Lake, Indiana, USA.

[16] For a defence of the Traditional or Received Text, see J W Burgon, *Revision Revised* (Collingswood: Dean Burgon Society, reprint 2000); E F Hills, *The King James Version Defended* (Des Moines: Christian Research Press, 1984); and Waite, *Defending the King James Bible*.

[17] For the intentional corruptions of God's Word found in the Alexandrian manuscripts, see J W Burgon, *The Causes of Corruption of the Traditional Text* (Collingswood: Dean Burgon Society, reprint 1998).

[18] Waite, *Defending the King James Bible*, xii.

[19] Burgon, *Revision Revised*, 16.

[20] For a critique of modern versions based on the Westcott-Hort Text, see Jeffrey Khoo, *Kept Pure in All Ages: Recapturing the Authorized Version and the Doctrine of Providential Preservation* (Singapore: FEBC Press, 2001), 69-100.

[21] Kurt Aland and Barbara Aland, *The Text of the New Testament* (Grand Rapids: Eerdmans, 1987), 102.

[22] See Carsten Peter Thiede and Matthew D'Ancona, *The Jesus Papyrus* (London: Weidenfeld & Nicolson, 1996).

[23] See Aland and Aland, *The Text of the New Testament*, 91.

[24] Erwin Nestle, Barbara and Kurt Aland, eds, *Novum Testamentum Graece*, 27th ed (Stuttgart: Deutsche Bibelgesellschaft, 1979), 246. See Theodore Letis, "The Strange About-Face of the New American Standard Version," Institute for Renaissance and Reformation Studies, January 9, 2002, in www.holywordcafe.com/bible, accessed on February 11, 2006.

[25] See chart on the two streams of NT Greek Texts in Jeffrey Khoo, *KJB: Questions and Answers* (Singapore: Bible Witness Literature, 2003), 9.

[26] See Jeffrey Khoo, "A Plea for a Perfect Bible," *The Burning Bush* 9 (2003): 1-15.

[27] Roy E Beacham and Kevin T Bauder, eds, *One Bible Only?* (Grand Rapids: Kregel, 2001), 121 (emphasis mine). See my critique of this book, "The Emergence of Neo-Fundamentalism: *One Bible Only?* or "Yea Hath God Said?" *The Burning Bush* 10 (2004): 2-47.

[28] Ibid, 114-5 (italics mine).

[29] Robert J Sargent, "A Scribal Error in 2 Chronicles 22:2? No!," *The Burning Bush* 10 (2004): 86-92. See also Chester Kulus, *Those So-Called Errors: Debunking the Liberal, New Evangelical, and Fundamentalist Myth that You Should Not Hear, Receive, and Believe All the Numbers of Scripture* (Newington: Emmanuel Baptist Theological Press, 2003), 367-8.

[30] James B Williams and Randolph Shaylor, eds, *God's Word in Our Hands: The Bible Preserved for Us* (Greenville: Ambassador Emerald, 2003), 361 (italics mine). See my critique of this book, "Bob Jones University, Neo-Fundamentalism, and Biblical Preservation," *The Burning Bush* 11 (2005): 82-97.

[31] Matthew Poole, *A Commentary on the Holy Bible,* (Mclean: MacDonald, nd), 1:542. See also Kulus, *Those So-Called Errors*, 222-5.

[32] Jack Moorman, *Modern Bibles—the Dark Secret* (Los Osos: Fundamental Evangelistic Association, nd),

LESSON 10

SUMMARY NOTES

QUESTION-AND-ANSWER SESSION

Chairman: Pr Dennis Kwok

Panelists: Rev Dr Jeffrey Khoo, Rev Dr Quek Suan Yew, Rev Dr Das Koshy

Summary notes by: Carol Lee

Question 1: I believe in VPP but I don't think it is serious enough for me to leave the church that believes otherwise. Am I wrong? Is believing in VPP a personal conviction?

Answer: <u>Rev Koshy:</u>

It is not serious enough for you to leave your church if your conviction is not contradicted or opposed by your church.

But if your church does not allow you to defend the truth, then it becomes very difficult for you to continue in your church.

Is VPP a serious doctrine? Most certainly. Without preservation, we would not have God's inspired words. And anyone can say this or that is his preferred reading, and not agree with the KJ translators' choice of Hebrew and Greek texts. It would be a matter of opinions then.

My conviction is that if VPP is denied so strongly as unbiblical and a heresy, you don't want to stay in that church and be called a heretic all the time.

Believing in VPP is a personal conviction because it is a doctrinal truth. It is not a preferred idea or opinion. It is God's truth.

<u>Rev Quek:</u>

If you are a church leader, you have to make it known to your fellow leaders your position because it is a very serious doctrine.

If you are just an ordinary church member, your leaders may be ignorant so you must let them know the truth. If they persist in their position, and you do not leave the church and continue to teach VPP, you will be undermining the church leadership or sowing seeds of discord and that is wrong even if your doctrinal position is right. If you stay and keep quiet about VPP, your conscience will bother you when your fellow church members (your children included) are taught that the Bible has mistakes. Your tithes and offerings will be used to promote that the Bible has mistakes since they do it willingly and openly and are not ignorant.

Question 2: Is VPP a new issue that arises in this millennium?

Answer:

<u>Rev Quek:</u>

The doctrine of preservation is not a new doctrine simply because it is taught in the Bible. It is as old as the Bible. The issue is new in the sense that there is a new attack on an old doctrine. And we have to defend this old doctrine. In our defence, we have to use words, adjectives (eg: "verbal," "plenary") to tighten the doctrine so that it will not be misunderstood, abused, misapplied, misinterpreted.

For example, when the doctrine of inspiration was not under attack, we never used the term "verbal plenary inspiration." But when the doctrine of inspiration was attacked, fundamentalists defended it and extra-biblical terms ("verbal," "plenary") were used to ensure that the attack will have no hold in the hearts and minds of the flock that God has placed in your care to feed.

It is not a new doctrine but a new attack on an old doctrine.

Dr Khoo:

The allegation that it is new doctrine comes from Bob Jones University and Central Baptist Theological Seminary. These schools do not believe that God has preserved His words 100%. They say that the doctrine of preservation is not based on the scripture. And if we cite Psalm 12:6-7, Matt 5:18, 24:35, they will very conveniently explain away these verses.

They will say they believe in the doctrine of inspiration and the infallibility of the autographs in the very beginning when it was first given. And they will say that now there are small insignificant mistakes in the Bible that will not affect our salvation. And that this is not important.

They say that VPP is a new doctrine that came about in 1648 when the Westminster Confession of Faith (WCF) was written. The WCF states that "God by his singular care and providence has kept his word pure in all ages." Quoting Matt 5:18.

Those who attack the doctrine of preservation quote Matt 5:18 but do not believe in it and apply it only to the commandments of God and not to every jot and tittle of God's words. They say it is an exaggeration to apply to every jot and tittle. The doctrine of preservation is considered a new doctrine by these so-called "scholars" in certain seminaries in the United States which do not believe in the preservation of the scriptures.

We Bible-Presbyterians believe and subscribe to the WCF. It is very surprising to me that B-Ps (who uphold the WCF and the Reformed Faith) are agreeing with people that attack the WCF and say that VPP is a new teaching and are attacking Scriptures that support the 100% preservation of the Word of God. Why must we here adopt and accept what they say? I can't understand.

Question 3: What is wrong with the belief that the Bible is preserved in the totality of manuscripts (or body of manuscripts) which includes the Westcott and Hort (W/H) critical texts?

Answer:

Dr Khoo:

The doctrine of VPP tells us that God has continuously preserved His words. No words are lost. All the words are kept intact to the jot and tittle and are always in the hands of God's people. His people will always receive His inspired and preserved words. The question is where these preserved words are.

Some say that the words are in the body of manuscripts (over 5,000 New Testament manuscripts). This body of manuscripts can be divided into two streams of manuscripts:

(1) The Preserved Stream: This consists of the majority of the 5,000 NT manuscripts and is the Preserved Line of manuscripts.

(2) The Corrupted Stream: This consists of a minority of the 5,000 NT manuscripts, represented by Aleph, A, B, C and D (five manuscripts). W/H hailed these minority manuscripts in the corrupted stream as the best. Dean Burgon (the contemporary of W/H) showed by clear study and investigation that these five minority manuscripts in the Corrupted Stream were scandalously corrupt. It is very difficult to find two verses in these manuscripts that can agree with each other. Yet they used these to "correct" the manuscripts that were received by the church as God's preserved words, that were used by the Reformers, and that were used by the KJ translators.

W/H changed the preserved texts and cut away 9,970 words, words that the church has been using all the ages. Egs: the last 12 verses of Mark, the verses in John 7:53 to 8:11 (on the adulterous woman), 1 John 5:7 (on the Trinity). These are God's preserved words that the church has received. Can we accept W/H as part of the preserved texts? If we say yes, it means that we have been using the wrong Bible all along!

W/H are unbelievers who do not believe in the inerrancy of scriptures. They were friends of Darwin and Freud, and were secret worshippers of Mary. They considered the first three chapters of Genesis to be myths and not history.

So, we cannot include the W/H texts as among the preserved manuscripts because they are different from the majority of the preserved texts.

Rev Quek:

Believing that the preserved words of God are in the body of manuscripts is an untenable position. If we believe in the doctrine of preservation, then we must have the words of God with us. If words are lost and we do not have them, then we cannot say we believe in the doctrine of preservation.

If we say the preserved words are somewhere in the body of manuscripts and start to use Higher Criticism to find these words, how do we know that what we find are really the words of God since we do not know what are the words of God in the first place? When we see two verses are different, how do we decide which is the word of God and which is not?

Be very careful of this deadly approach. We are not talking about a book of man, but The Book of God. The Bible can transform a child of darkness into a child of light, The Book that affects the eternity and the souls of people. If we say the Bible has mistakes, it will shatter our people's faith!

We do not play God. God is so powerful. Is He not able to preserve His own words? We must be aware of the deadly, diabolical proposal. It is subtle and laced with doctrinal arsenic. We must not swallow it. If we swallow it, we will die a slow death.

Question 4: Would it be difficult for Christians who are using a Bible translation that is based on the corrupt/minority texts to subscribe to the doctrine of VPP?

Answer:

Rev Koshy:

They will never come to a conclusive decision whether they have God's Word completely in their hands. These scholars don't agree on one text. They will keep wondering which text is the correct text. For example, our Kenyan brethren use the Kalenjin Bible which is based on the W/H text. When I preached from the KJ Bible, they realized that something is amiss. They can believe in the VPP if they are willing to look into the KJB and then translate from the Hebrew and Greek texts underlying it in time to come.

I do not think that if you use a translation that is based on the W/H text, you cannot believe in VPP. Anybody can believe.

Rev Quek:

The issue of preservation and the issue of translation are different issues.

The preservation issue is an issue about the Hebrew and Greek words preserved by God regardless of your language or translation of the Bible. You can believe in the Hebrew and Greek texts underlying the KJ Bible even if you do not have a Bible in your own language.

As for the choice of a Bible translation, it is about choosing the most faithful, most accurate translation. In using the word "most," it means that I must have something to compare with. That is: most faithful, most accurate compared to what? Compared to the Hebrew and Greek words!

The English Bible has a 500-year history. While we say that the KJ Bible is the most faithful, most accurate translation, we are not saying that the Chinese Bible, the Kiswahili Bible, and every other Bible have mistakes. Every translation must be measured against other translations in their own language to see which is the most faithful and accurate translation that they have. To make this measurement they must believe in the doctrine of VPP. The preserved texts underlying the KJ Bible are the texts preserved by God's singular care throughout the ages and finally identified for us by the KJ translators.

When the English Bible first came about by Tyndale, it was not a complete Bible. But people know that there are 66 books in the Bible. The English Bible took 500 years to develop to its present state.

Any Christian reading any translation can believe in VPP.

Dr Khoo:

If a Christian truly understands VPP, he will not use the W/H text or translations that are from the W/H texts because he can recognize that the text has many words left out. He will want all the words of God.

Rev Koshy:

In the church that has only the Kalenjin Bible, the members should seek help from their pastor and teacher to help them understand the differences. They can still believe in VPP.

Dr Khoo:

Jonathan Langat, a Kalenjin, did his thesis for his MDiv degree on updating the Kalenjin Bible based on the preserved texts. This helps his people to have all of God's words in their own language. Work has been done in this area.

Question 5: There are differences within the preserved texts. How do we know which is correct?

Answer:

Dr Khoo:

Based on the Logic of Faith, E.F.Hills in his book "The King James Bible Defended" starts with the promises of Christ that His words will be kept intact, that is, no words will be lost. This will lead us to the majority manuscripts and then to the printed text, the Textus Receptus (the Greek words underlying the KJ Bible). The identification is based on the Logic of Faith which is based on God's promises.

Rev Koshy:

We can't go back to check every manuscript, every word. God has already used His servants to identify the right words all through the centuries. Godly men have to come together to study and to give us the texts.

We need not look at all the manuscripts and come up with God's Word. God has already preserved His words for us. Just apply the Logic of Faith.

Dr Khoo:

Which edition of TR? We do not talk in terms of which text or edition of the TR is being preserved. Rather, preservation is the preservation of the WORDS of God: the Hebrew, Aramaic and Greek words behind the Reformation Bibles.

(The 16th Century Reformation is a great and miraculous event of God. Philip Schaff says that the Reformation is next to the Pentecost. Through it, the true church is separated from the false church. There was a return to the study of the biblical languages. The printing press was invented at that time which allowed for the production of the printed texts.)

The Trinitarian Bible Society (TBS) has also identified the preserved words of God as the Hebrew and Greek words underlying the KJ Bible: the Ben Chayim (not Stuttgart) text and the Scrivener's text (which is a combination of Beza's 1598, 5th edition and the Stephanus' last 2 editions). According to TBS, the words underlying the KJ Bible are the definitive reading. We do not need to change any words today. Our Hebrew and Greek Bibles are fixed.

From these Hebrew and Greek words, translations are to be made into the languages of the world so that people can know all the words of God. For us English Bible users, we use the KJ Bible as it is most faithfully and accurately translated.

Question 6: Is it true that 1 John 5:7 is not found in the Majority Texts but in the Latin Vulgate?

Answer:

Dr Khoo:

1 John 5:7 teaches the doctrine of the Trinity. This clear proof text is found in the TR and the Latin Vulgate. It is not that we do not have Greek evidences. We have Greek manuscript evidence of the presence of 1 John 5:7.

There is also internal evidence as we study the grammar. If we remove 1 John 5:7, the grammar will not fit. Both external and internal evidences point to the accuracy of 1 John 5:7. Theologically, it is a most wonderful verse. The verse that glorifies God must be right. God's word will never demote Christ.

Question 7: Some say that the text underlying the KJ Bible is a virtual text because it came into being only after the KJ Bible has been completed. It is considered "reverse engineering."

Answer:

Dr Khoo:

Jesus says He will preserve all His words. We just believe that all His words will be preserved. If God is the One who preserves, then we believe that the infallible and inerrant Hebrew and Greek words underlying the Reformation Bibles best represented by the KJ Bible are the preserved words of God.

This "reverse engineering" kind of talk is too technical for the lay person. We have God's infallible and inerrant words. And we have the most accurate English translation of these words. We do not have to invent or create words. We have the God-breathed words and they are kept pure by God.

Our logic must not work backwards: so many "errors," manuscripts, "mistakes," therefore the Bible has mistakes. Instead, we must begin with God's Word. No where in the Bible does it say that God's Word will be imperfectly preserved or lost. Dr George Skariah has exegeted more than 50 passages of God's Word that teaches us of God's preservation of His words. Begin with God's Word and it will lead us to the right conclusion.

Question 8: The KJB TR is the closest to the original is the original B-P stand. Have we shifted away from the B-P stand? How can "closest" mean exact?

Answer:

Dr Khoo:

Does "closest" mean there are mistakes? No where in the B-P church history did we say that the Bible has mistakes.

If "closest" means that our Bible is not infallible and not inerrant, then it is a wrong understanding.

We have to go back to the Bible. Psalm 19:7: "The law of the LORD is perfect, converting the soul: the testimony of the LORD is sure, making wise the simple."

"Closest" does not mean there are mistakes. "Closest" simply means although we do not have the autographs (tables of stone, the papyrus, the parchment), we have the same words, ie. the exact words although not the same tables of stone. The tables of stones are no more but we have the exact words. No autographs but we have the apographs. The B-P Church never held to the position that the Bible has errors.

Rev Quek:

Even if some say "closest" means mistakes, and we say "closest" does not mean mistakes, are we not playing a semantic game?

Sometimes we cannot cling on to tradition and use it as the basis for our beliefs as if tradition is engraved in stone and we cannot let it go. If tradition is wrong, we must change and not continue to hold to it. If tradition is right, then keep it.

When I first joined the B-P Church, no pastor, elder or deacon told me that the Bible has mistakes. Even today, our Basic Bible Knowledge class notes never said that the Bible has mistakes. No one dares to put it into our BBK notes that the Bible has mistakes because they can't defend their position.

If there were mistakes, can they list these mistakes? Does it mean that if these mistakes are corrected, we will have a perfect Bible?

So far, those who reject VPP have misinterpreted our position again and again to give themselves a bit of credibility.

They have not written any paper to defend their position. They made statements of what they do not believe, but never on what they believe. This is because they cannot demonstrate from Scriptures (not even from logic) to defend their position. Positional statements should state what one believes, not what one does not believe.

Question 9: Is the TR as old as the Bible? Or has the TR existed since the first century or for the last 400 years only?

Answer:

Rev Quek:

We must not confuse the actual possession of the TR with the identification of the TR.

Eg: The first century Christians already possessed the 27 New Testament books, but these were identified for us only in the 4th century.

Similarly, the TR was already in existence but not identified till later.

Why were they not identified earlier?

My suggested answer is that God knew that earlier there was no printing press. Only after the invention of the printing press, God used His people (through King James's sanction) to identify for us His preserved words and from them they gave us the KJ translation.
God's providential hand is at work: Paul went west and not east. The printing press was invented. The KJ team was a team of gifted translators, never to be repeated. English is today's international language. The British Empire spreading her influence all over the world with the English language is no accident.

Today, so-called scholars (of less than kindergarten standard compared to the KJ translators) want to decide what should be in the Bible and what should be out. Who are they? Are they advocating sacerdotalism, that they are people with secret knowledge? This is absolutely subjective. How can we believe them?

But if God has preserved His words, and we have His preserved words, we have to stop using the deadly method of textual criticism to criticize God's Holy and Perfect Word. We must just accept God's words.

Dr Khoo:

It is not human identification but divine identification.Preservation is by God's singular care. How? God is a God of history. He works through history. In the days of the Reformation, God gave us the printed text, with all His words intact. Matthew 4:4: "But he answered and said, It is written, Man shall not live by bread alone, but by every word that proceedeth out of the mouth of God."

Do our words today go back to the day of Moses? To the New Testament time? Yes, the Hebrew and Greek words underlying the KJ Bible go back to Moses and to the New Testament time. And this is based on God's promise. I take God at His word, by faith.

Hebrews 11:6: "But without faith it is impossible to please him..."

"It is written." It was written. And it will always remain written. The Greek word is in the perfect tense. It remains perfectly written.

If God can preserve my salvation, He can preserve His words.

Kept pure? Never disappear? Yes, He is all powerful.

Hebrews 11:6: "...he is a rewarder of them that diligently seek him." He has preserved His words for us. We are to diligently seek Him through His preserved words. And He will reward us. This is a matter of faith otherwise it will not please Him.

APPENDIX

MORE ARTICLES ON THE DEFENSE OF THE BIBLICAL DOCTRINE OF VERBAL PLENARY PRESERVATION OF THE BIBLE

You will need Adobe Acrobat to read some of these articles, which can be found at:
http://www.febc.edu.sg/Doctrine%20of%20Perfect%20Preservatio n.htm

- A 21st CENTURY REFORMATION MOVEMENT FOR THE VERBAL AND PLENARY PRESERVATION OF THE HOLY SCRIPTURES (Jeffrey Khoo)

- A BOOK REVIEW OF D. A. WAITE'S "DEFENDING THE KING JAMES BIBLE" (Dennis Kwok)

- A CHILD OF GOD LOOKS AT THE DOCTRINE OF VERBAL PLENARY PRESERVATION (Carol Lee)

- A CRITIQUE OF *GOD'S WORD IN OUR HANDS: THE BIBLE PRESERVED FOR US* (Thomas M Strouse)

- A HISTORY OF MY DEFENCE OF THE KING JAMES VERSION (Edward F Hills)

- A MORE SURE WORD (Stephen Khoo)

- A PERFECT BIBLE TODAY! (Jeffrey Khoo)

- A PLEA FOR A PERFECT BIBLE (Jeffrey Khoo)

- A PUBLIC RESPONSE TO MR LIM SENG HOO'S OPEN LETTER AND PAPER AGAINST THE VERBAL PLENARY PRESERVATION OF SCRIPTURE (Jeffrey Khoo)

- **A REVIEW OF JACK SIN'S ARTICLE, "A GRAVE MATTER: VERITY, SAGACITY AND CLARITY IN THE TEXTUAL DEBATE"** (Biak Lawm Thang)

- **A SCRIBAL ERROR IN 2 CHRONICLES 22:2? NO!** (Robert J Sargent)

- **A SERIOUS WARNING TO THE CHURCH TODAY** (Wang Ming Tao)

- **A STANDARD RAISED** (Timothy Tow)

- **ARE THE LAST TWELVE VERSES OF MARK REALLY MARK'S?** (Jeffrey Khoo)

- **BEARING TRUE WITNESS** (Jeffrey Khoo)

- **BIBLICAL AUTHORITY** (Jeffrey Khoo)

- **BOB JONES UNIVERSITY AND THE KJB: A CRITIQUE OF *FROM THE MIND OF GOD TO THE MIND OF MAN*** (Jeffrey Khoo)

- **BOB JONES UNIVERSITY, NEO-FUNDAMENTALISM, AND BIBLICAL PRESERVATION** (Jeffrey Khoo)

- **BRUCE METZGER AND THE CURSE OF TEXTUAL CRITICISM** (Jeffrey Khoo)

- **CAN VERBAL PLENARY INSPIRATION DO WITHOUT VERBAL PLENARY PRESERVATION?: THE ACHILLES' HEEL OF PRINCETON BIBLIOLOGY** (Jeffrey Khoo)

- **CANON, TEXTS, AND WORDS: LOST AND FOUND OR PRESERVED AND IDENTIFIED?** (Jeffrey Khoo)

- **CLARIFICATION OF CONFESSION** (Brutus Balan)

- **CONTENDING IN TRUTH, AND TRUTH AFFIRMS THE VPP OF SCRIPTURE** (Jeffrey Khoo)

- **CORRECTIONS TO THE NEW TESTAMENT OF THE CHINESE UNION VERSION IN LIGHT OF THE PRESERVED TEXT BY JAMES SUN** *(PDF 718 KB)*

- **DEATH IN THE POT!** (Timothy Tow)

- **DID GOD PROMISE TO PRESERVE HIS WORDS?: INTERPRETING PSALM 12:6-7** (Quek Suan Yew)

- **DID GOD WRITE ONLY ONE BIBLE?** (Jeffrey Khoo)

- **DID JESUS AND THE APOSTLES RELY ON THE CORRUPT SEPTUAGINT?** (Prabhudas Koshy)

- **EARNESTLY CONTEND FOR THE FAITH** (Timothy Tow)

- **EXCEEDING GREAT AND PRECIOUS PROMISES** (Prabhudas Koshy)

- **FAITH GUIDES, INTELLECTUALISM BEGUILES** (Prabhudas Koshy)

- **GOD'S PROMISE TO PRESERVE HIS WORD (PS 12:5-7)** (Shin Yeong Gil)

- **GOD'S PURITY OR MAN'S PERVERSITY—WHICH?** (Denis Gibson)

- **GOD'S SPECIAL PROVIDENTIAL CARE OF THE TEXT OF SCRIPTURE** (Timothy Tow)

- **GOD'S WORD ASSAILED BY THE FATHER OF LIES** (S H Tow)

- **GOD'S WORD FOR THE END TIME** (S H Tow)

- **GOD'S WORD IS PERFECT AND PURE, SURE AND TRUE (PSALM 19:7-10)** (George Skariah)

- **GOD'S WORD IS SETTLED FOR EVER (PSALM 119:89)** (George Skariah)

- **GOD'S WORD: THE INCORRUPTIBLE SEED (1 PETER 1:23-25)** (Ephrem Chiracho Ouchula)

- **GOSPEL STRATEGY FOR THE NEW MILLENNIUM** (S H Tow)

- **HIS WORD ABOVE HIS NAME** (Jeffrey Khoo)

- **HOLY HATRED** (Timothy Tow)

- **IF WE REJECT THE DOCTRINE OF THE PERFECT PRESERVATION OF THE BIBLE** (Prabhudas Koshy)

- **INSPIRATION, PRESERVATION, AND TRANSLATIONS: IN SEARCH OF THE BIBLICAL IDENTITY OF THE BIBLE-PRESBYTERIAN CHURCH** (Jeffrey Khoo)

- **INSPIRED TEXTUAL CRITICISM?** (Jeffrey Khoo)

- **IS THE PRESERVATION OF SCRIPTURE A DOCTRINE WORTH DYING FOR?** (Michael Koech)

- **JESUS ON PERFECT PRESERVATION OF THE BIBLE** (Quek Suan Yew)

- **JESUS' VIEW OF THE HOLY SCRIPTURE : AN EXPOSITION OF MATTHEW 5:17-19** (Prabhudas Koshy)

- **JOHANNINE COMMA - 1 JOHN 5:7-8 (A PRELIMINARY EXAMINATION OF THE ANTIQUITY AND AUTHENTICITY OF THE JOHANNINE COMMA)** (Jeffrey Khoo)

-
- **JOHN OWEN ON THE PERFECT BIBLE** (Jeffrey Khoo)

- **JUDGES 18:30: MOSES OR MANASSEH?** (Quek Suan Yew)

- **KICKING AGAINST THE PRICKS: THE SCCC CONTRADICTS THE ICCC ON VPP** (Jeffrey Khoo)

- **LESSONS ON THE DOCTRINE OF VERBAL PLENARY PRESERVATION** (Truth B-P Church)

- **LOST WORDS IN OUR BIBLE?** (Jeffrey Khoo)

- **MARK THEM WHICH CAUSE DIVISIONS** (Paul Ferguson)

- **MAKING THE WORD OF GOD OF NONE EFFECT** (Jeffrey Khoo)

- **MISTAKES IN THE BIBLE?** (Jeffrey Khoo)

- **MODERN DENIAL OF PRESERVATION** (Lawrence E Bray)

- **MULTIVERSIONS ONLYISM** (Jeffrey Khoo)

- **MY GLORY WILL I NOT GIVE TO ANOTHER (ISAIAH 42:8)** (Timothy Tow)

- **MY REPLY TO JAMES D PRICE'S REVIEW OF "A PLEA FOR A PERFECT BIBLE"** (Jeffrey Khoo)

- **NIV CLAIMS EXAMINED: A CLOSE LOOK AT TODAY'S BESTSELLER** (S H Tow)

- **NIV TURNS "LAND OF SINIM" INTO "REGION OF ASWAN" BY A TWIST OF THE BALL-PEN!** (Timothy Tow)

- **NO PERFECTLY PRESERVED WORD OF GOD TODAY?** (Tan Kian Sing)

- **NON-RUCKMANITE ANSWERS TO ANTI-KJB QUESTIONS** (Jeffrey Khoo)

- **OUT VPP GNAT, IN ASM CAMEL** (Jeffrey Khoo)

- **PERFECT BIBLE NOT PERFECT VERSION** (Jeffrey Khoo)

- **PRAISE GOD, BEREAN B-P CHURCH HAS A PERFECT BIBLE TODAY!** (Tan Kian Sing)

- **REFORMATION INTO THE TWENTY-FIRST CENTURY** (Timothy Tow)

- **REVISIONISM ANCIENT AND MODERN** (S H Tow)

- **"SET FOR THE DEFENCE OF THE GOSPEL"** (S H Tow)

- *SOLA AUTOGRAPHA* OR *SOLA APOGRAPHA*?: A CASE FOR THE PRESENT PERFECTION AND AUTHORITY OF THE HOLY SCRIPTURES (Jeffrey Khoo)

- **THE BATTLE FOR THE KING JAMES BIBLE IN THE BIBLE-PRESBYTERIAN CHURCH** (S H Tow)

- **THE BIBLICAL DEFENCE FOR THE VERBAL, PLENARY PRESERVATION OF GOD'S WORD** (Thomas M Strouse)

- **THE BIBLICAL DOCTRINE OF THE VERBAL, PLENARY INSPIRATION OF GOD'S WORD** (Jack Sin)

- **THE CANONISATION AND PRESERVATION OF SCRIPTURE** (Jeffrey Khoo)

- **THE DEAN BURGON OATH** (Jeffrey Khoo)

- **THE EMERGENCE OF NEO-FUNDAMENTALISM:** *ONE BIBLE ONLY?* OR "YEA HATH GOD SAID?" (Jeffrey Khoo)

- **THE INSIDE STORY OF WESTCOTT AND HORT**

- **THE INTERNATIONAL COUNCIL OF CHRISTIAN CHURCHES (ICCC) AND THE KING JAMES BIBLE** (Jeffrey Khoo)

- **THE KJB-NIV DEBATE by Jeffrey Khoo** *(PDF 731KB)*

- **THE NECESSITY AND NEEDS OF A BIBLE COLLEGE** (Jeffrey Khoo)

- **THE NUMBERS IN EZRA 2 AND NEHEMIAH 7: A SOLUTION IN FAVOUR OF THE INERRANCY OF THE VERBALLY AND PLENARILY PRESERVED TEXT** (Nelson

Were)

- **THE PROVIDENCE OF GOD** (Jeffrey Khoo)

- **THE REFORMATION BIBLE** (Jeffrey Khoo)

- **THE STORY OF THE ENGLISH BIBLE** (Jeffrey Khoo)

- **THE TRANSLATORS' AWESOME TASK** (S H Tow)

- **THE UNFINISHED COMMISSION (MATT 28:18-20)** (Timothy Tow)

- **THE WOMAN TAKEN IN ADULTERY (JOHN 7:53-8:11)** (Jeffrey Khoo)

- **THREE HEAVEN AND EARTH MOVING STATEMENTS FROM GOD'S MOUTH SETTLE THE QUESTION WHETHER HIS WORDS ARE PRESERVED** (Timothy Tow)

- **TO DRAW A SNAKE AND ADD LEGS**

- **TO MAGNIFY HIS PERFECT WORD** (Gia-Hien Nguyen)

- **TRINITARIAN BIBLE SOCIETY, VERBAL PLENARY PRESERVATION, AND THE TEXTS UNDERLYING THE AUTHORIZED VERSION**

- **UNDERMINING GOD'S WORD BY SUBTLE STUDY BIBLES** (Jeffrey Khoo)

- **UNTRUSTWORTHINESS OF THE NIV** (Jeffrey Khoo)

- **VPI AND VPP: DOES IT CONCERN ME?** (Boaz Boon)

- **WHY ONLY KJB?** (Jeffrey Khoo)

- **WHY WE SHOULD REGARD THE BIBLE AS AUTHORITATIVE** (Prabhudas Koshy)

- **WILL OUR B-P SONS DEFEND THE FAITH?** (Jeffrey Khoo)

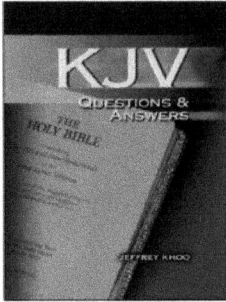

KJB Questions & Answers by Dr Jeffrey Khoo

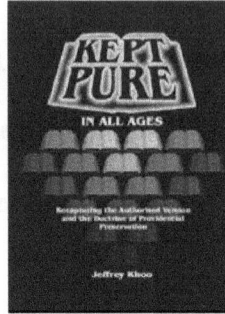

Kept Pure In All Ages by Dr Jeffrey Khoo

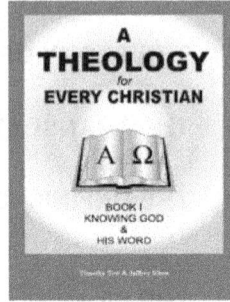

A Theology For Every Christian Book 1 by Rev Timothy Tow & Jeffrey Khoo

INDEX

Order Blank

Name:_____

Address:_____

City & State:_____Zip:_____

*Credit Card #:*_____*Expires:*_____

Latest Books

[ ] Send 2 Timothy--Preaching Verse by Verse, by Pastor D. A.
    Waite, 250 pages, perfect bound ($20+$5 S&H) fully indexed.
[ ] Send *A Critical Answer to God's Word Preserved* by Pastor D.
    A. Waite, 192 pp. perfect bound ($11.00+$4.00 S&H)

The Most Recently Published Books

[ ] Send *8,000 Differences Between Textus Receptus & Critical
    Text* by Dr. J. A. Moorman, 544 pp., hd.back ($20+$5+ S&H)
[ ] *Early Manuscripts, Church Fathers, & the Authorized Version*
    by Dr. Jack Moorman, $18+$5 S&H. Hardback
[ ] Send *The LIE That Changed the Modern World* by Dr. H. D.
    Williams ($16+$5 S&H) Hardback book
[ ] Send *With Tears in My Heart* by Gertrude G. Sanborn.
    Hardback 414 pp. ($25+$5 S&H) 400 Christian Poems

Preaching Verse by Verse Books

[ ] Send 1 Timothy--Preaching Verse by Verse, by Pastor D. A.
    Waite, 288 pages, hardback ($11+$5 S&H) fully indexed.
[ ] Send *Romans--Preaching Verse by Verse* by Pastor D. A. Waite
    736 pp. Hardback ($25+$5 S&H) fully indexed
[ ] Send *Colossians & Philemon--Preaching Verse by Verse* by
    Pastor D. A. Waite ($12+$5 S&H) hardback, 240 pages.
[ ] Send *Philippians--Preaching Verse by Verse* by Pastor D.
    A. Waite ($10+$5 S&H) hardback, 176 pages.
[ ] Send *Ephesians--Preaching Verse by Verse* by Pastor D. A.
    Waite ($12+$5 S&H) hardback, 224 pages.
[ ] Send *Galatians--Preaching Verse By Verse* by Pastor D. A.
    Waite ($12+$5 S&H) hardback, 216 pages.

Send or Call Orders to:
THE BIBLE FOR TODAY
900 Park Ave., Collingswood, NJ 08108
Phone: 856-854-4452; FAX:--2464; Orders: 1-800 JOHN 10:9
E-Mail Orders: BFT@BibleForToday.org; Credit Cards OK